Typ &

Greetings —

a word about Lent
at Christmas

McNeill

Dec 1939

THESE SHARED HIS PASSION

These Shared
His Passion

STUDIES IN THE LAST WEEK
OF THE LIFE OF JESUS

by

EDWIN McNEILL POTEAT

HARPER & BROTHERS PUBLISHERS

THESE SHARED HIS PASSION

Affectionately Inscribed
to my sisters

PRISCILLA

ISABELLE

CLARISSA

ACKNOWLEDGMENT

The author wishes to express his appreciation to the following authors and publishers for permission to quote from their copyrighted works: From *Atoms in Action* by George Russell Harrison, William Morrow & Company, 1939; from *Not Peace, But a Sword,* by Vincent Sheean, copyright 1939, Doubleday, Doran and Company, Inc.; from *Every Man's Life of Jesus,* by James Moffatt, and *The Clue to History,* by John MacMurray, Harper & Brothers; from *Rudyard Kipling's Verse, Inclusive Edition 1885-1932,* by Rudyard Kipling, copyright 1891, 1934, reprinted by permission of Mrs. Rudyard Kipling and Doubleday, Doran and Company, Inc.

Thanks are due Mrs. Walter Rauschenbusch for permission to use Walter Rauschenbusch's poem "The Little Gate to God"; and to the following periodicals for permission to use the material indicated: *The British Weekly* for permission to reprint from "The Veil Was Lifted" by Robert Buchanan; *The Christian Century* for permission to use a selection from an article by Arthur E. Holt; *Harper's Magazine* for Josephine Johnson's poem "In This Stern Hour"; *The Cleveland Plain Dealer* for permission to use the poem "Have I Not Been Here So Long," from Ted Robinson's column, *The Philosopher of Folly*; and *The American Magazine* for permission to quote from "The Seekers" by Victor Starbuck.

CONTENTS

Certainly there are difficulties in the gospels themselves, difficulties which no amount of honesty and moral sympathy can solve, and about which many people have not time to think. Some things are uncertain that we would like to be certain; other things are obscure, as any ancient history is liable to be, at this distance of time. Learned persons debate such points, but the story is for more than learned persons, and a dozen difficulties do not blur the impression made by the personality of Jesus upon the unprejudiced mind. He stands out, real and commanding. There is enough authentic and original material to exhibit his life as it was lived on earth actually and vividly. Those who have studied the gospels technically have cleared away a number of obscurities, and although we still see darkly at this point and that, on the whole the records have become more luminous as they have been analyzed. It is now fairly practicable to trace the outline of the tale of Jesus behind the different traditions and to recover the salient features of the main narrative that shimmers through the four biographies which we call gospels.

INTRODUCTION

The quotation on the facing page is from the Prologue of *Every Man's Life of Jesus*[1] and is used here because the chronology followed in these studies is Dr. Moffatt's. He has put together the story of the life of Jesus with due regard for the relation of the synoptics to the Fourth Gospel; and in quoting the language of the Master, he makes the scholar's use of what best fits the total picture.

The point to be remembered is—as he says: "the story is for more than learned persons, and a dozen difficulties do not blur the impression made by the personality of Jesus upon the unprejudiced mind. He stands out, real and commanding."

The object of the following chapters is not a critical one. Rather they are written in the hope that they will add somewhat to the command and the realism with which the Gospels endow the personality of Jesus. The wealth of detail with which the last week of the Lord's life is recorded is due, in part, to the heightened tension of those days. With dramatic suddenness things began to happen; and the drama was over before its audience, and those who played its thrilling roles, realized it. But out of that acceleration and tension was born the greatest movement of human history.

Those who came within the sweep of those cyclonic events were many. It would be impossible to analyze the experiences of all who shared his passion. There are, however, certain figures, without which the story would have been far less dramatic than it turned out to be. And some of these players are significant not alone in themselves but also in the way in

[1] James Moffatt. *Every Man's Life of Jesus* (New York: Harper & Brothers).

which they set forth the impact of those six days on certain vital and enduring human experiences. Indeed, it is the author's feeling that all of the characters discussed here are representative of the conflict that Jesus sets up in every heart that confronts him.

The home at Bethany gives us a picture of a perpetual struggle between two aspects of vigorous and effective living; the Greeks in the temple become the focus of the conflict between two irreconcilable spiritually dynamic principles; Thomas is the picture of the bewilderment of one who confronts one of the most baffling of all life's questions; and Philip is no less so as he worries over another. James and John are the prototype of the conflict between spirit and flesh; and the place of fear as a primary spiritual drive is seen in the denials of Peter, the treachery of Judas, and the cowardice of Pilate.

The stories that introduce each chapter are designed to give a setting for the discussions. If there is a use of minor fragments of the record that is unauthorized by a strict following of the text; or if as other bits are put together they do not fit into the familiar pattern of the Gospels, such liberties are taken only in the interest of giving vividness and actuality to the atmosphere of mind and event in which the drama is conducted.

These shared his passion, and with him had a part in creating a situation that brought into the record of humanity six days that changed the destiny of the race, six days during which, as Moffatt puts it, he stood out, real and commanding. Surely there is nothing that can reduce either his reality or his sovereignty to those, who in these latter days likewise share his passion.

THESE SHARED HIS PASSION

Chapter I: MARY AND MARTHA

THE HOME IN BETHANY

Martha stood in the low door, narrowed her eyes defensively against the sharp sunlight, and looked out into the court. It had been a very hot day, one of those early spring assaults of heat that bring sudden warning that summer's long burning days are soon to settle their blight on the fresh cool colors of the spring. A large sycamore tree, its trunk splotched like the flesh of a leper, shaded one corner of the yard with oblique patterns, and waved its wide leaves listlessly over the narrow gate.

She was a rather tall woman; at least her thin angular figure suggested height unusual among the women of her race. Once lovely to gaze upon, she had grown careless of her appearance; dark eyes that once were bright with the eagerness of youth were now dull with the shadows of fatigue and loneliness. She brushed a wisp of hair from her forehead with a tired hand, and wearily leaned her head against the jamb of the door.

All day long she had waited the arrival of the Teacher of Galilee. He had sent word by an early pilgrim to the Passover, that he would rest at Bethany the night before the festival crowds began to converge upon the holy city. Since early morning the little house had been tidied up. Fresh linens and a lily from the border of the stream below the hill, brightened the guest chamber. A new wick rested in a saucer of clear oil, and wheat cakes, crisply browned, and golden honey freshly strained, waited only the guest's arrival to be served. Even after all the needed preparations were complete, Martha had puttered nervously about, multiplying her chores by needless repetitions, and fretting endlessly at the Master's delay.

Within the dark and cool interior of the house, Mary, younger than Martha by twelve years, reclined indifferently on a couch. Such enterprise as the day had demanded of her had been met with attention to her own person. She had massaged her lovely face with fragrant oil, and draped a gaily colored garment about her in soft, copious folds. As she stroked her hair with careful fingers she hummed snatches of song, or smiled wanly in a newly burnished mirror, as vagrant recollections returned to animate the somber deeps of her eyes. Street sounds drifted over the wall and into the window, half-opened since the air outside had begun to stir. Pilgrims were passing on their way into the great city. All day their shuffling feet had raised clouds of yellow dust; and as they went along the melody of the ancient songs of their people broke from their lips with the carefree lilt of holidaymakers. Every now and then the curt, imperious admonition of a donkey driver was emphasized by the thwack of his stick on the rump of his beast; and the grunt of a camel registered a futile protest against the spasmodic jerkings that communicated, along the length of rope to the wooden pin that pinched his nostrils, the impatience of his custodian.

"Mary." The voice was high pitched and querulous, but Mary did not answer. All day long her older sister had called to her in rebuke or command, and all day long Mary had found it safer to be silent than to speak.

"Mary, the Master comes; I hear him knocking at the gate."

She sat up, and tossing her head, freed the long mantle of hair that fell like a fragrant shadow across her shoulders and down her back. Out in the hot courtyard she heard Martha's greeting in words that while cordial were touched with gentle reproach; and heard Jesus explaining that his delay was due to unexpected ministries demanded of him by travelers on the Jericho road. As they neared the door Mary observed her sister's uneasy efforts to arrange her disorderly hair, and plucking an oleander blossom from the spray on the table, she toyed with it gracefully as she went forward to greet the visitor. Martha looked sharply at the flower and then at her sister. There was studied contempt in her deep intake of breath and dilating nostrils.

"These have been unhappy days," Martha was complaining. "Lazarus stays late in the city. He likes not the stares of these stupid villagers, and thinks they plot some evil, even as they threatened you when you were last here. He is hopeful his little booth by the south wall, where he sells hard bread and sweet wine, will earn him some extra money. We need it sorely these days."

"Yes," replied Jesus with an upward inflection of his quiet voice.

"Yet if they learn at Jerusalem that he is walking death ——"

Mary stood in the door and greeted Jesus modestly.

"Sit here," ordered Martha, "where it is shady. I shall fetch water for your feet and—" Her voice trailed off into inaudible chatter as she pushed past Mary and shuffled to the low dark kitchen.

Jesus sat down heavily on a stone settle by the wall, and kicked off his dusty sandals with an accustomed toe-against-heel movement. Mary stepped backward into the house as Martha entered, and from a shelf near the door picked up a vase of nard. As she returned to the court, she lifted the glass stopple and released a wisp of pungent fragrance, and then, with a movement as deft as it was unexpected, she knelt, and poured the sweet unguent over the visitor's tired feet, massaged them vigorously for a moment and then dried them tenderly with her luxuriant hair.

"That's better than water and a napkin," she said pleasantly.

As she was rising from her knees, Martha appeared in the door. She stood for a moment in astonishment, but said nothing, and turning quickly, went inside again.

The twelve disciples had followed Jesus into the yard and set about at once to refresh themselves by turns at the large water jar that stood under the eaves near the corner of the house. Martha had not expected so large a company, but gave no indication of her dismay at seeing them. Instead, when she saw that the honored guest was likely to suffer no neglect while Mary was around, began amplifying the preparations already made to meet the emergency demand.

"And are they many who are coming to Jerusalem?" The voice was Mary's. She had settled herself comfortably near the seat where Jesus rested.

"Yes, and they seem wilder than ever with their expectations of the holiday. How refreshing it is to escape from the din and furor of the road into this haven of silence and repose. I am reminded here how easy it is for us to lose the meaning of life by trying to give meaning to it. These pilgrims live from year to year for this week of festival. And yet the riot of holiday-making depletes their strength, frays their nerves, wastes their scant store of money, and sends them home weary and irritated and ——"

Martha interrupted his words by appearing suddenly in the door. She extended her hands, palm outwards in a gesture of annoyance. Her fingers glistened with golden oil, and she was girded with a serving apron. For a moment she looked appealingly to the pair who returned her stare, and waited for a word from him. The men in the yard looked at her casually.

"Will not *you* ask her," Martha said, irritation giving edge to her words, "to come in here and help me? All day long I have slaved to make this poor house decent enough to welcome you, and she has only ——"

Jesus looked from Martha to Mary, but there was no reproach on his face, and when his glance returned to Martha, pity showed in his soft, sure eyes.

"Martha, Martha, you have cumbered yourself about with much serving. Mary has chosen the better part, and it will not be taken from her."

THE BETTER PART

We shall not understand the passion of our Lord if we fail to sense the tension of those six short days that shook the world. Nor shall we adequately appraise the words and acts of those who shared his passion except they be seen against a background of strain and apprehension.

Here in the household at Bethany, we encounter the first case of nerves. There was tension in the family circle. The only man in the house had been sick, and had died. Few things create an atmosphere so definitive as illness and death. The constant vigil, the effort to insure quiet and induce rest, the hurried consultations, and the anxious use of medicament followed by torturing moments before effects can be observed, the recurrent hope and returning despair, and then death. There follow the kindly ministries of friends, well-intentioned always, but not infrequently officious and annoying; the bewilderment about plans and the need for hasty preparations for burial, details with which one has had no experience. And then the agony of separation and the final relinquishment of the one beloved to the indifferent earth.

It was not enough that the breadwinner of the Bethany household had died. There was that moment when hope was stirred that he might live if only the Galilean could be persuaded to come and heal him. That expectation had been unaccountably denied. He would not respond; mysteriously he declined to come back to the house. But strangest of all was the aftermath. Something happened—we shall never surely know what—and Lazarus was returned to the family. But it did not quiet the tumult or give healing to the stricken hearts of the house. The villagers were outraged by the incident. They laughed, or they ridiculed, or they scorned. When they saw the sick man restored and in their midst again, they

avoided his presence and cried out evil epithets that made him
retreat in confusion and shame. And Martha, who had cared
for him as he wailed deliriously in sickness, tried now to comfort him as he whimpered in resentment, feeling all the while
that little of the pity and much of the scorn of the villagers
was transferred from him to her, deepening her own sorrow.

Martha's temperament may have been little help to her.
The elder of the two sisters, and the one on whom the cares
of the household rested, she was perhaps jealous of the younger
Mary. Kipling, within the typical bourgeois framework of his
generation, pictured Martha as the mother of the workers of
the world, and Mary as the mother of the idlers who live by
the toil of their less fortunate brethren.

The Sons of Mary smile and are blessèd—they know the angels
   are on their side,
They know in them is the grace confessèd, and for them are
   the mercies multiplied.
They sit at the Feet—they hear the Word—they know how
   truly the promise runs.
They have cast their burden upon the Lord, and—the Lord
   he lays it on Martha's Sons.

This insight is too shallow. It is more likely that Martha was
the nervous, activistic type, fussy, restless and repressed; and
that the placid nature of her sister and her garish reputation
afforded her neither rest nor solace. For Mary, young and
beautiful, had early determined that life would not frustrate
her with the deadening routine of domestic and invalid cares.
And if she had exploited her temperament as a courtesan,
it was no more than Martha had done as a drudge. But all
the wiles of the seductress, the perfume, the extravagance of
toilet and dress, the arrogant indolence, these were as abrasives
on the nerves of her jealous sister, a jealousy that sought to
compensate itself with an ostentatious busyness, by which

Martha vainly hoped her resplendent sister would be rebuked. Here was a situation set for friction, a circumstance that invited acrimony or sullen silence.

But the guest of the late afternoon, had also entered into a period of spiritual tension. The holiday spirit gripped him with its excitement; the capricious crowds intrigued his interest and stirred his hopes. There had been quarrels and even threats of rebellion among his disciples, and he had been forced to wonder if he could hold them steady through the days immediately ahead. "Simon, Simon, Satan hath desired thee—but I have prayed that thy faith fail not." The leaders, already hostile, were growing bold and threatening. It was no longer likely that an open break could be avoided. And what if a treacherous impulse should mature to action in his intimate circle! There were hours of inner conflict, moments of anguished prayer and furious self-examination. He was soon to be thrown into an act of reckless courage in the temple, alone and unaided; he was to see a crowd arise like a mist and envelop him with wild acclaim, only to dissolve and leave him alone and hungry beside a fig tree that beckoned with its leaves, but offered no fruit. This was the state of mind he brought to Bethany. The nation, the village, the family, and the friend were all emotionally taut.

If we do not sense this, we will not understand the approval he gave to Mary's mood. To Martha, Mary was shamelessly lazy. Indeed, it is not hard for us to agree with Martha's impatient request for help. It does not seem quite fair that Mary, instead of meeting an emergency, should have met the guest with a studied and even insolent disregard of her domestic responsibilities. The reason we tend to side with Martha and deplore ever so mildly Jesus' complicity in Mary's shirking, is that we live in an age when the display of physical activity is the sign of man's nobility; and when leisure is cognate to laziness. We must be muscular and mobile. The athletic torso and the high-powered motor are the symbols we exalt in our virile and velocitous age. Activism is dignified by a philosophy that has taken its name. Its opposite is suspect until one is too old to work. We do not object so much to what Mary did; we object to her doing it. It would have been quite all right for Mary's grandmother, but Mary should have been in the kitchen.

Thus we seem to question whether Mary's was the better part. And yet we must not allow our distrust of laziness to blind us to a very important fact. It is possible that we who are familiar with this story have missed its point by the words that create the picture. "The better part" sounds opportunist, like the seizure of an advantage. It sounds as if, as Kipling represented it, life is either drudgery or dreaming; and he is better off who, by accident or shrewdness, finds himself exempt from work.

But this is an inaccurate idea, based on an inaccurate translation of an interesting word. The Greek word *meridzo* means to divide or apportion or assign. And *merida* means therefore an assignment. It carries with it as definite a connotation as duty. A clearer rendering than the accustomed one would be: Mary has chosen the more important assignment.

This at once changes the atmosphere surrounding Jesus and Mary from one of indolence and purposelessness, to one of deliberate and discerning participation. In the nature of the case, two needs had to be met. One was concerned with physical restoration, the other with spiritual relaxation. Martha was sure—she could not have been persuaded otherwise, her temperament being what it was—that the more imperative need was for food. So she cumbered herself—the word actually means "an outward expression of mental agitation"—with many things. It was a deeper understanding of Mary's, aided also no doubt by her temperament, that what was necessary was the exact opposite of agitation; quietness-and-repose, that was the one thing needful. Of course, if we wish to be unkind to Mary we can insinuate that her intuition was that of the courtesan. But is it not fair, and in the light of the commending word of Jesus, is it not imperative indeed to assume that it was the insight of one who, under his influence, had found a higher level for the exercise of love, and expressed it with the protective emphasis that met perfectly the need of the moment?

Our picture actually presents Mary active in the performance of a very important duty, one she was fitted to perform. She might have made a mess of the meal. Certainly Martha would have helped matters little if *she* had sat at his feet. One can think of the stream of anxious questions Martha might have poured forth, anticipating every possible mishap in the kitchen, and imagining a thousand calamities elsewhere that would never occur. For herself, for the situation in the home, and for the guest, Mary had selected the better assignment. For in the light of the next six days, what the friend of the family needed then, more than a meal, was rest and relaxation in a quiet place, with an understanding person who would wait for his silences as eagerly as for his words. Mary saw more clearly and deeply than Martha. Hers was the better part.

It is not hard for us to see that the tension of those days made such a time of quietness "the one thing needful." We shall be discovering as we go along that it was a consciousness of this need and a constant effort to meet it that was the unique resource of Jesus during the last week. We have called it variously the Spirit, the sense of God's presence, spiritual power, and what not. He called it the Better Part; and his possession of it accounts for some of the difference of poise and self-control that separated him from the panic and terror of those who shared his passion. To Mary, who made it possible for an hour at the close of a crowded day, goes the award of the ages. "Wherever the gospel is preached throughout the whole world this also that she hath done shall be spoken of for a memorial of her." "She hath done what she could."

We are beginning to discover that, in our modern world, Mary's act is still needed, and grows increasingly so. The tension of the last six days of our Lord's earthly life was terrific; and yet, there is no disputing the fact that it can be matched by fiercer tensions in almost any six days of our times. During the past five years, War, the Great Destroyer, with devilish cleverness developed a new technique. Instead of declaring, it threatened war. This created an agonized suspense that hung like a cloud over vast populations, who waited for the explosion that was week by week postponed. Such deliberately fostered tension was duly christened "the war of nerves," and since its inventor was conspicuously national-socialist, it was presently refined to "Nazi-nerves." But it is not discriminatingly used. The residents of Paris and London had Nazi-nerves before the declaration of war in September, 1939; and the people of Germany and Eastern Europe have had them longer than that. And now America is growing mildly irritated—a condition which we are warned is preliminary to nervousness. The whole world is neurotic, and—if we are to judge by what seems to be going on—the chancellories of the nations are occupied by jitterbug diplomats. This affords us a new element to guide us in any appraisal we may make of the widely unexpected political and diplomatic *revanches* of the past twelve months.

The ominous increase in nervous diseases and the efforts to provide for the care and cure of the mentally ill, the tide of restlessness that moves upon the world, the multiplying uncertainties that fester in the homes where nerves are raw, in industry where quarrels are rife, in government where bickering is the essence, instead of the spice, of parliamentarism—it is a sorry picture, even if these lines are drawn in incomplete and somewhat distorted perspective. When fatigue was once called the great killer, the ingenuity of inventive minds was requisitioned to create mechanical slaves to do the drudgery. Today the work of this country might be done in four three-hour days if we could make use of all the tools provided. But the prospect of the leisure such a program would suddenly create for millions whose nerves are so geared to routine that they run wild when released—this prospect actually deters the shortening of labor hours. In his *Technics and Civilization* Lewis Mumford has sketched the process of mechanical development and its influence on health. The discovery, a century or less ago, that farmers lived longer than industrial workers, gave pause to the few far-seeing men who found it out. Neotechnics called to their aid the biological and psychological sciences. Studies of working efficiency and fatigue proved that a curtailment of hours would increase production per unit. Leisure turned out to be the ally of profit, instead of its enemy, and improvement in working conditions was reflected in improvement in bank accounts. But the blessings of such advance have not been unmixed. The displacement of workers by technological improvements has created a volume of unemployment that is one of the largest culture beds of psychic disorder today; and the exploitation of leisure by commercialized entertainment has substituted the quest for a good time for the cultivation of the spiritual resources by which man ultimately lives. It has come to pass that when men, who are employed on public works projects, rest momentarily on their shovels, their pause becomes a national scandal and Congress begins shaving its budget down to meet only the needs of the congenital activists.

Thus we are confronted by a medical problem of enormous proportions. Our neglect, by the very organization of our daily lives, of "the better part," has made us sick, despite the advances made in the medical sciences and in the treatment of organic illnesses. *Time* of August 28, 1939, reports a Harvard neurologist as announcing that the x-factor, hitherto unknown in arthritis, is "poverty, grief and family worry." The incipience of "tough times, no work, family discord," correspond in point of time with the onset of arthritis. The column heading carrying this medical discovery was entitled "psychic arthritis"!

It costs dearly also in the field of art. The acceleration of life and the loss of the capacity for rest, reflection, and that serenity of spirit that is the parent of creativity, results in the grotesqueries of modern daubing that goes for painting in certain sophisticated circles. Why waste three years on a portrait that can be smeared in an hour? If art critics, whose tastes to some of us seem psychotic or even mildly mad, will acclaim a polychromatic mess as a creation of a new type of the painter's art, why take pains. It is easier to give them. And what of music? Statistics is a poor guide in the estimate of the real sensitiveness of a people to music; and yet the incredible popular interest in and demand for "hot" tunes and "whacky" rhythms inclines one to fear that the multiplication of those latest freaks of nature—cats, ickies, and alligators—is already quite out of hand!

Is not the staccato or telegraphic prose of the new novelists after all a degenerate literary offspring of a once noble and aristocratic language? Perhaps it is pressing matters too far, but it is increasingly evident that our lack of relaxation, and our frantic misuse of leisure is exacting a toll that is paid not only by our heart valves and arteries, but by all the components of our general culture. So long as the set tendency and quality of our life is tense, so long as it is easier to take a cocktail or a cigarette for jittery nerves, than to spend an hour in physical and mental repose; so long as sedatives are convenient and advertised as omnipotent, just so long will the art of relaxation elude us and the inclination to recover it be feeble. Little wonder then, that when, taut with anxiety or fear we are plucked by a crisis, we vibrate with panic and so easily destroy each other and ourselves. He was interested in more than in merely turning an aphorism who recently said that tension is the only unpardonable sin. There is precedent for such an observation. If anger is anterior to murder, is not nervous strain anterior to anger?

The amazing fact is that such a condition is only lately come upon us. The loss of Sunday, with its vast therapeutic powers, is very recent. The arrival of the five-day labor week is even more so. I recently found a letter written by my father when he was in college. He found no difficulty adjusting himself to life in 1937, but when he was eighteen he was rebuking himself mildly, as the letter disclosed, for having written to his mother on Sunday! As recently as that, the day was regarded as a time for nothing save the rest and recreation of the spirit. Compare that with Sunday now. Today the admonition is: Don't write—telegraph!

It would certainly be a strange crusade, the mind of the world being what it is, that set out to convince the world of the practicability and the primary need of "the better part." For one of the aspects of the psychosis that afflicts us is our obsession with its opposite. Therefore, there can be no reorganization of life in the large that will make a return to serenity of spirit mandatory. Nothing short of a chaos so complete that the very patterns of modern life would be destroyed, and even the recollections of its magnificence and power lost, is likely to displace our culture for one that exalts the primacy of spiritual resources. But this does not mean either that we must abandon our faith in "the better part," or that we must wait hopefully for the destruction which will clear the way for it. Much the same situation exists as that which characterizes the recent retreat from the social gospel by certain liberals. While we deplore the modern drift that makes the cultivation of the spirit difficult, we must, nevertheless, seek mental relaxation within the context of our everyday lives. We need, this is to say, to be converted to habits and practices as individuals that will lessen the strain that life, in the main, creates. It is not enough to read a book on how to make friends and keep them. We need to discover how to make friends with our own souls, and to keep them. And no wiser word has been spoken than the ancient one which admonished a generation that knew not a tithe of our tension: "In quietness shall you possess your souls."

This is being done, of course, by some who have sensed the need. The difference between arriving at his office rested by his morning drive, instead of unnerved by it, was described recently by an automobile commuter, as simply a matter of his momentary relaxation at the red traffic signals. Instead of sitting tense, with both legs and arms rigid at their mechanical duties, he slips the transmission into neutral, and slumps comfortably for twenty restoring seconds. Some have adopted variations and adaptations of Yoga; and there is available for those who seek, instruction in physical exercises which carried out are guaranteed to palliate the pain or the exhaustion of nerve tissue.

But it is, after all, a concern for spiritual poise and power that has always been one of the primary emphases of religion. It may have been an over-emphasis; but we are out of range of that danger now. If in our Christian faith and practice we have been so seduced by the sirens of activism, that we have turned our backs on contemplation and the practice of the mystical art, it is time that we were warned about it. Not only must corporate worship provide for spiritual relaxation; Christian people must somehow be made to recognize it as a duty they owe themselves and their neighbors. It is not difficult for those who will, to discover "the little postern gate"[1]

[1] These are only three verses of the longer poem.

THE LITTLE GATE TO GOD

> In the castle of my soul
> Is a little postern gate,
> Whereat, when I enter,
> I am in the presence of God.
> In a moment, in the turning of a thought,

that the late Walter Rauschenbusch wrote so beautifully about. It is a reproach that we must bear that the man, who by the observance of a weekly day of absolute silence has developed spiritual powers that have literally shaken the world, is no member of the Christian fellowship, but a pagan!

The obvious point of all this is that because in an ancient day, Mary did what she could, and what she saw was very important, she made possible a measure of that superb physical and spiritual strength in which Jesus walked through the tenseness of his testing days. If we have lost her insight into life, or if we scorn to do what we can, we shall not enable others, who look to us for guidance, to walk through anxiety and danger with a steady tread; and if humanity finally loses its will-to-relax, it will lose its balance and ultimately go mad.

Is there then not some message that the Christian church can bring to these days, some Mary-ministry it can perform? We invite those who pass our doors to come in and rest and pray. But to the sanctuary

> Of plinth and bending arch and groin,
> Where light and half-light sifting through,
> Where flame to kindling flame can join
> To purge the soul's dark residue,

there are few who come, and they steal in and out as if hopeful

---

> I am where God is.
> This is a fact.
>
> This world of ours has length and breadth,
> A superficial and horizontal world.
> When I am with God
> I look deep down and high up,
> And all is changed.
>
> The world of men is made of jangling noises.
> With God is a great silence.
> But that silence is a melody
> Sweet as the contentment of love,
> Thrilling as a touch of flame.

that their strange behavior will escape detection by the more robust passers-by. This is surely a day of new and terrible passion. No area of life is exempt from its anguish, and no sensitive and perceiving soul wishes to escape it. But it is also a day of new and enchanting hope if we choose the one thing needful, accept the better assignment, the better part.

A certain man, who is widely recognized as eminent in the fields of business, church and general culture, was asked by a friend to name what single factor had accounted for his extraordinary success as a person. This was his reply: "I have made it a practice for many years to have a half hour each day after breakfast for relaxation. Even my routine is relaxed, for I have nothing I must do for these moments, but let myself go. During those periods more problems have been solved than in conference, more insights into life have visited me, more of the sense of God has possessed me."

That was the one thing needful—that surely is the better part.

Chapter II: THE HOUSE OF PRAYER

SOME GREEKS WERE THERE

It was the sixth hour of the day, the short three-hour interval between nine and twelve in the morning. In the Court of the Gentiles, four men, dressed in the distinctive garb of Greek travelers, sat alongside the barrier that separated them from the Court of the Priests. Above them, in their own familiar tongue, a sentence cut in the stone wall warned ominously: "No stranger is to enter within the balustrade round the temple and court. Whoso is found will be guilty of his own death to follow."

One of the men, in appearance younger than the rest, was talking vigorously though it was obvious he was keeping his voice low.

"My house shall be called a house of prayer for all nations. Is this not the word of Jehovah? And what about the vision of the peoples of the earth gathering on Mount Zion; is there not such a boast among these bigots?"

"Quiet, Sosthenes, you will be heard; such words will raise a barrier between these folk and us thicker than this stone." The speaker laid his hand on the balustrade as he spoke his quiet warning.

"Truly," continued the young man, "but is it not strange that we should come to the temple of the Most High God only to learn of the narrowness of the human heart? The temple of Diana is open to all; and nowhere will you find a hateful word like this on its walls. We who are revolted by the worship of lust come hither to seek true worship, only to find God denied us because we are 'strangers.' Little wonder the priestesses of Diana have boasted that the shrine of Venus is more hospitable than the altar of Jehovah."

The conversation lapsed momentarily when a lad moved slowly toward them, scrutinizing carefully the cracks that separated the broad paving stones in the courtyard. Suddenly he stooped and with a sharpened stick salvaged a small coin. It was a Greek drachma and, after a quick examination he held it up enthusiastically for the strangers to see. Then he drew four other coins of varying worth from a small wallet, counted them studiously as if reflecting on what sort of trinket they would buy, and then returning them to the purse, resumed his search.

"There was a Galilean in here yesterday morning who had this court in an uproar for a few minutes. It was before you came."

"Yes," said young Sosthenes, "I heard about it. After seeing this warning here, I could wish I had been here to help him clean the rabble out."

"But it was not the rabble," corrected the older man. "It was the money-changers and the vendors of sacrificial animals. That lad is profiting in his small way from the reckless scattering of coins. You would scarce believe it now, but yesterday at this time, this court was as empty as the holy of holies. The men who fled before his fury were back again as soon as he left the temple; but for a while there was the wildest confusion, followed by a strange calm, that lasted more than an hour."

"But why was he not restrained by the temple guard, or set upon by the worshipers?"

"Well, the soldiers seemed to delight in the riot, and since it subsided almost as quickly as it began, they really had no problem on their hands. As for the people, they were astonished at first; and then they too seemed to take perverse pleasure in the discomfiture of these hucksters whose reputation as cheats is, as you know, a by-word among Passover pilgrims."

"Why does he not return today to repeat his purge? The job needs finishing."

"That I cannot say. He may come back again. This is about the time he and his friends entered the sanctuary yesterday."

"I remember," said Sosthenes, "a fracas once in the temple of Diana, back home in Ephesus. It too was in the morning. I happened to be passing the great portal when a mob of priestesses and trinket-sellers came stampeding into the temple concourse. There was no making out what the cause of their confusion was. Everybody was yelling and nothing appeared as urgent as the necessity for getting away from some pursuing fury. I am not one to linger about looking for trouble, so I made my way off quickly in an opposite direction. It was the talk of the city the next day that a fanatical priest of Mithra had slipped into the sanctuary of Venus, and after calling on the goddess to aid him, ran through the temple, screaming about an impending doom, laying about him with a short club which he used indiscriminately on souvenir-monger and vestal alike."

"What happened to him?"

"I never heard. The incident was soon forgotten; and the next day there was no evidence of what had happened the day before."

"I am not surprised," responded the older man. "Such things happen every now and then in nearly every city. Corinth seems to make a practice of it; but the temple only grows more and more corrupt. I wonder if it does any good. Is that the way to cleanse a place of its refuse of corruption? To brandish a whip and threaten, even though the threat be in words of ancient religious wisdom—is it thus that the hearts of men are purified, or their deeds made righteous?"

"It may be," interrupted one of the men who up to this

point had not spoken, "that this sign here that set Sosthenes off is another way of keeping the spirit pure. For some of the ancient prophets of Israel, the gathering of all peoples in Jerusalem was a dream of great beauty. But for the common mind, such a dream is dangerous. The peoples of the world who come to Mount Zion bring with them their dreams too, and one dream often corrupts or cancels another. It was a more practical mind, I think, that cut these words for strangers to read. We do not like them, to be sure, and yet . . ."

"And yet you would say that the way to keep religion pure is to keep it free from contacts with strange peoples?" This was the voice of the fourth Greek.

"Yes, I think it is. If one is not to be driven to such violence as yesterday's, one must anticipate corruption and keep it out."

"But they were no strangers to Israel who yesterday fell under the Galilean's wrath. The last man of them was a Jew. You couldn't have set up a money-stall if you had wanted to. We are the aliens, not they."

"Indeed; but are there not those who say that it is alien influence that has turned the worship of the pilgrims into a source of profit to the rulers of the temple?"

"That I know not; it is a good excuse, in any case, for those to make who have turned this sanctuary into a robber's stronghold."

The crowds were growing steadily in the broad court. The stalls for cattle were already filled, and money-changers' tables were ranged along the wall in the shaded areas. Worshipers were haggling over currency exchanges, and the noise of bargaining filled the air.

Presently a slight commotion was observed at the Gate Beautiful. A small group of peasants, led by the Galilean, entered the court. There was a magic hush that silenced every sound for a moment, as all eyes turned toward him. His hand was empty; he carried no whip but his face was clouded with displeasure. Those who the day before had cringed and fled before his anger waited now to see if he was about to descend upon them again. A money-changer near the gate swept with a frightened movement his neat piles of coins into a leather wallet. A seller of doves reached inside a wicker cage and began feeling for a grip on the blue legs of his fluttering stock. But the Galilean paused only for a moment, and proceeded toward the court of the priests.

"Here he comes," said Sosthenes, pointing in the direction of the gate. "He is back to cleanse the court again."

"No," said the older man, "I think not. His face is unhappy today; yesterday it was angry. Grief, not fury, possesses him today."

The little group moved toward the balustrade, and was about to enter the inner court. Two of them, lingering behind, stopped for a moment a dozen steps from the opening. Without a word of consultation with his friends, Sosthenes stood up and stepped hurriedly toward them, and with a short and unceremonious greeting accosted the one nearest him.

"Sir, we would see Jesus."

Philip stared incredulously at the Greek, and without the courtesy of a reply, turned and spoke to the man who stood at his side. Andrew did not answer; instead, his eyes wandered to the balustrade and ran along the warning to strangers, cut imperishably in the stone.

Sosthenes, despite a touch of embarrassed resentment, politely repeated his request; whereupon the two men turned as if impelled by a single idea, and re-joined the Galilean's crowd. Philip pushed his way into the center, and plucking Jesus' sleeve, whispered the strange request into his ear.

"Now is the time for the Son of Man to be glorified," he answered. Then he looked back, and when Sosthenes bowed in greeting, he smiled, and turned, making his way slowly back toward the balustrade.

"I am Sosthenes, of Ephesus, come hither to worship. For many years I have looked forward to the time when I might come into the presence of the true and living God, in this holy city of your people."

"It is good that you have come," replied the Galilean.

"But," protested the Greek, "a barrier is set against our worship, we cannot enter . . ."

"God is a spirit and they that worship him; worship him in spirit and in truth."

"Truly spoken, Teacher. And yet what worship, what truth, what spirit is there in this mercenary confusion?" Sosthenes waved his hand in a broad half-circle, pointing to the business which had been noisily resumed after Jesus had passed. "Is there more danger to true worship in us, or in that? Yesterday you cleansed the court of this rabble; today we are denied entrance into the place of worship. Will you drive these people hence today? And will your people grant the sanctuary to us that we may worship tomorrow?"

Jesus looked at his questioner with a clear and motionless eye. For a moment he made no reply. The three companions of Sosthenes had joined their friend, and all of them stood awaiting an answer. The silence was awkward. Finally Jesus spoke, but his words seemed addressed to himself alone.

"Now is my soul full of trouble. What shall I say? Father, save me from this hour? Yet for this very purpose I have come to this hour. Father, glorify thy name."

There came a voice from the sky, "I have glorified it and will glorify it again."

The crowd that stood by and heard it said it had thundered. Others said an angel had spoken to him.

SOUL FULL OF TROUBLE

We are not likely to enter into the full meaning of the passion of our Lord unless we sense the tension of those six days that changed the direction of human history. We have been reminded that his need of relaxation at the Bethany home was occasioned by his knowledge of the growing hostility of the leaders, of the rifts appearing among his intimates, and of the capricious mind of a people on holiday, ready to crown a king or crucify a carpenter, according to the mood of the hour. And that he set for himself the deliberate task of lessening that tension in his own spirit and in the minds of his friends ("let not your hearts be troubled") is obvious from any reading of the record. The striking fact emerges as the story unfolds, that his poise and self-reliance seemed to grow as the days moved on and as his need became acute. The exact opposite was true of his friends whose final act in the tragic drama was ignominious flight into the darkness of the Garden of Olives. There must have been a direct connection between his calm and triumph, and between their excitement and defeat.

The evening at Bethany was a refreshing interlude, no doubt. But that brief renewal of spiritual energy was not enough to last for very long. In fact, the next day, the day that has been singularly miscalled a triumph, found him stormed by misgivings. Whatever else may be said for the story of his entrance into the city, this much must be said: it was a strange sort of triumph, judged even by the simplest standard. He called it no such thing; and one cannot think that he for a moment regarded the clamor of an indiscriminate rabble, however exalted may have been their hopes and however laudatory their hosannas, as a celebration of a victory, unless it was deliberately spurious, or a cynical caricature. If subsequent ages have pictured the day as one of great exaltation, it is because the scene remembered has been out of the life of David (as Matthew quoted it) and not out of the life of Jesus. And the obvious fact is that he behaved as little like a conqueror at the close of the day as he had at its beginning. He retreated to Bethany as evening fell. Was it because the hysteria of the crowd and the torture of his own spirit drove him again to a spot where quietness could win a spiritual victory, and repose be the only needed testimony of triumph? It is not difficult to answer such questions.

It was on Monday that he cleansed the temple. Few experiences in the life of Jesus have caused more dismay than this episode. This is attested by the devious ways in which explanations of it have been sought. The inference is that he was angry; but since we have not thought of him as an angry sort of person, even under the most cruel treatment, we have said his anger was righteous. But this helps us little, however it may save his reputation. How are we to know when *our* anger is righteous and when wicked. For twenty centuries the phrase "righteous indignation" has been, like patriotism, the last refuge of many a scoundrel. Jesus violated property rights, deliberately and without recompense to those he despoiled. This, we hasten to explain, was due to a sense of right and property higher than the rights of pedlers and petty bankers. He used force in a vehement and immoderate fashion. This is the thorniest of the problems raised. To contemplate him deliberately weaving a whip of small cords, fully knowing it was to be used to expel from the temple court those he was to call robbers—this is a painful picture indeed. So we have affirmed that he "drove" the cattle only, and implied that his attitude toward the offending humans was conciliatory or definitely gentle. He turned the other cheek to the money-changers while he turned their tables over. One has the feeling that such explanations if ingenious are overly so. We must find an interpretation that is consonant with our general picture of him. If we would like him better with this episode deleted, we must either delete it, or leave it intact and adequately accounted for.

For this reason we return to the atmosphere of acute spiritual tension as the one in which such a thing might naturally happen. If he was truly angry, and resorted to unwonted physical violence, let us admit it and explain it not as righteous indignation, but as taut and quivering nerves. In the plexus of confusion and strain we can see the picture clearly, and explain it with fairness to all the elements in it.

As he came into the city in the morning, he met the disappointment of the fruitless fig tree. Renan explained his curse on the tree as the resentment that hunger causes. A hungry man is a nervous man. We have demurred: Renan was wrong. But was he? There is surely no grave discredit in being petulant when one's nervous balance is disturbed by a disorganized food regimen. And if he had to go on into the city without food; and if he entered the temple and—still hungry —confronted the waste and the stupid bickerings over food that presently was to be consumed on sacrificial altars, is there any reason why he should not have rankled within?

There had been many times before when he had seen the temple profaned. Its unspeakable corruption had dawned on him long before the week of his death. Its open and insolent commercial exploitation of the worship impulse of simple and unprotected peasants; the emptiness of its formalism; the carousal, the sin—little wonder he called it a den of robbers; but why had he not thought of this before? It is hardly credible that he had *not* thought of it. In fact there is every reason to think that he had pondered long and painfully on it. And, we assume, up to this last week, he had deliberately avoided the use of threat or violence. It was John the Baptist who had thundered about the axe at the root of the tree. Jesus had utterly refused the terrorist methods that were the impulse of that amazing wave of repentance that swept like a freshet down the Jordan. John was bewildered by the gentle tactics of his successor, and when his own career was interrupted, sent messengers to ask about it. The reply about blind men seeing, and poor men hearing the gospel was hardly what he expected. We can see, without much strain on the imagination, John cleansing the temple; but Jesus toppling tables and calling names seems out of character.

And yet, if we recall the sense of tension, we are within reach of a plausible explanation of his changed mood. Add to the elements of strain that this Monday morning had already provided, the quick realization that, after the experience of the day before, the temple had become for him the precincts of peril. Already it had been hinted that if something were not done about it, the whole world would go after him. The visit of the disciples to Bethany had not restored confidence to the group. Judas had quarreled about Mary's extravagant waste of perfume. It was none of his business, and the rest of the group were quick to notice it and draw an ugly inference from his impertinent concern. Jesus must have felt the circle of hostility narrowing about him, and at the same time and for the same reasons, the circle of his dependable friends widening. The time for action was growing short. He must act now, and alone. He was not desperate, but things were not getting any better. Should he stake success on a quick, decisive, spectacular blow in which his concern for righteousness could be dramatized at the very point where God's spirit was thought to dwell?

This sort of thing had happened so many times before—the violence of the escape from Egypt under Moses' uncompromising leadership, for example—that it is exactly what we might have been led to expect had we anticipated the act, instead of looked at it after the lapse of many centuries. And it has happened so many times since, that we are almost compelled to assign, certainly as a part of the explanation, the terrific nervous drive that was moving the heart of Jesus in the direction of conclusive action. It may, to some, sound impious, and to others fantastic, to say that the cleansing of the temple was a case of nerves as much as an act of heroic devotion. And yet the clue to this estimate lies finally in the words he himself spoke shortly after the incident was over.

Before turning to his words, however, there are other considerations that confirm the judgment that he came soon to deplore his own rashness. It was a futile and unrealistic gesture. He had reflected before on Jerusalem, and the sight of its gilded dome as it broke on his sight when he once rounded the brow of Olivet had moved him to tears, not to fury. He had used a gentle figure of speech to describe his longings. He wanted to protect her from those who stoned prophets and killed God's messengers, as a hen protected her chicks under her wings. He knew that violence was poison, and he had said so repeatedly. Nor is there any evidence that this sudden vehemence did any good. The situation must have returned to normal very soon, and there is evidence that the corruption he struck at so rashly continued for nearly forty years until one of Titus' reckless soldiers tossed a burning torch into a pile of tinder and set fire to the sanctuary in the year 70.

Nor was such an act consistent with the principles by which he had organized his life and that of his followers. It was not necessary to worship in Jerusalem. Why then was it necessary to cleanse the sanctuary? If it were true that they that take the sword, perish by the sword, were it any less true that those who take the whip will suffer from the whip? There were some, said he, who would take the kingdom by violence, and there always had been. But such rashness was as mistaken as it was dangerous.

But it is when we look at the record of what he had to say, after his temper had cooled, that our clearest light breaks. The section of the record in John's Gospel that follows immediately the request of the Greeks for an audience with Jesus becomes lively with fresh interest when it is seen as following also close upon the temple episode. If what Jesus had to say be understood as reflections upon what had just happened, we cannot escape the feeling that he was making a contrast between what he had done in the temple and what was the guiding principle of godliness. "Except a grain of wheat fall into the ground and die," "He that loveth his life shall lose it," "If any man serve me, him will my father honor,"

"Now is my soul troubled; and what shall I say?" "Now is the judgment of this world: now shall the prince of this world be cast out," "And I, if I be lifted up will draw all men unto me." These sentences are among the most important in the whole New Testament, and from them endless inspiration has been drawn. But which of them reflects the furious atmosphere of the temple cleansing? None. If, in retrospect, he had been represented as soliloquizing in a vein of self-approval, he would likely have said: Death is no principle of life, he gets results who strikes hard; he that loves his life, fights for it; if any man serve me, the crowd will applaud his courage; there is no perplexity in my spirit now, I struck and the crowd scattered; that was the judgment of the world, and when the money-changers fled, the prince of the world was close on their heels; and if I am to draw the world to my way of living, it is the whip that will persuade it!

We have not been accustomed to this as we have read the story. We have been told that his word about his troubled soul was inspired by the sudden realization that the Greek world, represented by the visitors, might after all have been more hospitable to him than his own; that he was swept, for a moment, with a temptation to abandon Israel for Greece. But he had touched Greek life before, and may have even spoken the language somewhat. Certain it is that this contact, and the possibilities it is thought to have suggested, was no novelty. If the sight of Greeks had not perplexed his spirit before, why should it now? If, on the other hand, it was the prospect of the cross that troubled him, why his confidence that only in the death of the grain was fructification possible, and why his emphasis on the fact that by such an expedient alone was he to draw all men to him?

But if we can feel that these Greeks who shared his passion in ever so slight a way, were the immediate cause of his repudiation, after quiet reflection, of the rashness of an act committed the day before in a moment of great nervous tension and strain, we can enter, not only into a deeper understanding of his testing time, but participate—and this is more important—more perfectly in his experience.

Here is, after all, the crux of the matter. The tradition of the Hebrew people in their greatest day was a pacific one, despite numerous deviations from the noble ideal that their history records. The Greek mind was equally pacific to the extent, at least, that it found a glorification of the cult of violence, in individual or group, a poor second to the glories of art and philosophy. It is to these two great historic traditions that we turn wistfully when we are overwhelmed by the deification of violence which in our day has named new gods before whom we are expected to prostrate ourselves in fear or in resignation. The contest seems endless; indeed in the essential quality of human life there is found the element of this struggle. The balance is difficult to maintain between vigor and violence; between creative and destructive uses of power. That the difficulty was one Jesus encountered is only a further testimony to the fact that he was in all things tempted like ourselves.

Tempted like ourselves; and we might go on to say tempted like the rest of the world, for none is free from this colossal struggle. The heart of the world is full of trouble, perhaps as full at this hour as it has ever been. It has felt the thrill of victory, only to discover its conquest a spurious and empty thing. Armies have marched, and treaties been signed; nations have been born and boundaries set; religions have arisen and converts multiplied; books have been written and minds kindled. And yet we talk of the doom that impends. It is the same old tension, tightened—we seem to feel—to the snapping point.

And this troubled heart of the world is betrayed once again by desperation or terror into the futile business of plaiting whips with which it hopes to drive out the chicanery and the cruelty that corrupts the courts of our temples—temples of trade mostly, for that is our major concern, and we are told the economics is at the very center of our difficulty. And the church that twenty short years ago repented of its folly, is plaiting whips again. When the hot wind blows, the church will bless its whips as they go into action. For one of the tragic, if not the most tragic, facts of modern life is that while we have put crosses on our churches, we keep whips in the street. Rejoicing as one must in the progress that has been achieved in the last decade, it is still true that industry finds the whip its most potent weapon, and labor, conscious of its growing strength, plaits its whips and waits its striking hour.

One cannot help wondering what would happen today if the tension in life could be somehow relaxed so that men would lay aside their whips. For it is our conviction that men only reach for whips when some inner palsy has shriveled their courage, or some outer threat has inflated their fear. And once the whip has been raised it can hardly restrain or soften its blow. The cycle begins, and whip added to whip eventually will, some dolefully predict, embroil the world in an endless castigation.

This is no place to enter the limitless field that invites the inquiry of those who seek for an alternative for the whip. It is the point of this study that when Jesus confronted himself as a whip-wielder, his soul was sore troubled, and in a series of amazing sentences he repudiated the whole sorry and useless business. His concern for purity never abated, he never acquiesced in the sin and folly of the temple. He was not blind to the malice and greed of men. Within a few days he was to warn his adversaries that he could, if he would, mobilize twelve legions of angels to protect him, but even then he knew he would not, and they must have known it too. For whatever weapon the great and eternal enterprise of redemption was to employ, he was convinced at last that the whip of small cords had no more part in it in his day than the machine gun can have in ours. He was to be lifted up; it was not his to batter down.

. This is a hard lesson to learn; and we confess to its truth only when we have thrashed our enemies into temporary submission, and then, in a moment of heavy breathing, discovered that our own hands have been cruelly bruised in the process. We go to war, righteously; and the evil that our noble recklessness expels drifts back the moment our hands take respite from battle. The bells that rang for German victory in 1870, were melted for munitions in 1915; the councils at Versailles in 1919 were canceled by the concessions at Munich in 1938. And if we know, as we truly must, that the sin of the world cannot be driven out with a whip, that evil will not yield its life up to the terror that threatens or the hand that smites, why are we who talk of following Jesus so slow to drop our whips?

There are two answers to this. The tension under which we live makes us tighten our grip; and—the cross is harder. No man can accept the principle of the cross hysterically. It takes the quiet and the calm of trust in the ultimate ethical core of the universe to accept *that*. Tension and distrust, cannot we say that these two sinister influences pushed Jesus into his rash act on that fateful Monday morning? And what, indeed, but tension and distrust drives us into the rashness of our own days of passion?

"There were some Greeks there." This is an interesting sentence. These unnamed visitors stood at a watershed in the last week of Jesus' life. Did they induce by a question the conflict that shook his spirit? An answer to that can be nothing more than conjecture. "My soul is full of trouble." This is an important word. There we see the struggle fully joined. "Except a grain of wheat fall into the ground and die, it abideth alone; but if it die it bringeth forth much fruit." That was the answer; and having found it, he moved without detour to the hill of redemption, outside the city.

Chapter III: THOMAS

I remember," Nicodemus was saying, "the visit I had with him three years ago when he was here for the Passover."

Thomas sat quietly as was his habit, but his finger tips drummed nervously on his knee, and his eyes moved restlessly about the luxuriously appointed room where he and Nicodemus had sat alone for nearly an hour.

"He was just come from Galilee, and there was immense enthusiasm for him among the common people."

"Yes," assented Thomas, "he has a way with crowds, most of the time."

"In fact, he was quite the talk of the pilgrims that year. Wherever he went he had a following; and it was openly talked that he could, if he would, become a leader of nation-wide influence."

"I have never quite understood," Thomas put in uneasily, "why he has not followed up the advantage that his popularity gives him. He likes people, definitely, and a crowd is quick to discover his sincerity and friendliness. He even takes time to romp with children; and no man can number those who have felt his healing touch, or heard words of comfort from his lips."

"There is a story," Nicodemus observed, "about feeding a great multitude one late afternoon, by the lake. It has been told here in the city, greatly exaggerated perhaps, but we have wondered why he did not do that sort of thing more often. Certainly nothing secures a popular following like free meals." Nicodemus smiled pleasantly at the picture this brought to mind.

"Yes, so have we wondered," answered Thomas. "And yet,

you know, perhaps, that he left that crowd on the shore, and crossed the lake to get away from them?"

"No, that I had not heard. Did he explain why?"

"Not then, exactly. But on a similar occasion when the people thronged him, he told them that if they wanted to follow him they must deny themselves, and carry crosses. And so, naturally, most of them left off following him. I confess that even to me, his words seemed somewhat untimely, not to say impractical, or blunt."

There was a long silence between the men which neither seemed anxious to break. Both were thinking deeply, Nicodemus in a detached sort of way, and Thomas with a sense of personal stake in his reflections. It was about noon, and Thomas was in the home of the rich young friend in response to an invitation brought to him by a messenger as he was standing in the Court of the Priests. Nicodemus was still a young man, though his position in Israel because of his wealth and learning was more important than that of many of his elders.

"I think," Nicodemus said finally, "that I might have given my support to him if I could have been sure what he was up to. The first time I saw him, he said I needed to be born into the life of the spirit. It was a strange idea, at first, but I came later to see its truth. But when I met him the second time, he demanded that I sell all my goods, and follow him."

"Yes, I remember that time," said Thomas.

"But the two attitudes seem to be at cross purposes," Nicodemus went on. "If he is concerned with spiritual values, why should he bother with a distribution of wealth among the poor? Is poverty for me requisite to spiritual vigor; and is wealth for the poor necessary before they can be borne into the world of the spirit?"

Thomas did not answer for a moment, and then, leaning forward on his divan, replied with great earnestness:

"True enough; and you are not alone in your bewilderment.

I confess myself to much doubt about what he expects to do. I have heard him speak of the end of time as if it were soon to come to pass, and then to warn us against the error of thinking of such a thing. I have heard him speak disparagingly of the law of Moses, and then say that not one jot or tittle of it shall pass away. We started out with him as fishers of men; then we became the lights of the world; then sons of the Kingdom. He will not denounce Rome, neither will he accept political leadership. He seems apprehensive about this festival, yet insisted on coming. Three days ago he drove the hucksters from the temple; and the next day seemed to repudiate the act."

"Has he said in so many words what he expects to do? Where does he think his course will end? He has lost many followers already. Will he hold the rest of you? Would he still take away the wealth of the rich and distribute it, or does he aim at an enrichment of the spirit only?"

"I wish I knew," answered Thomas. "We have talked among ourselves about it. James and John think he plans a political movement and have sought for position in it. Judas of Kerioth thinks he has lost hope. I—I seem to grow more and more confused. And yet . . ."

"But he cannot expect that you will . . ."

"Follow him?" Thomas completed the question.

"Yes—follow him."

"I can only speak for myself. I came to Jerusalem this time even though I feared some evil might happen to him, and perhaps to us. My confusion somehow gave way before his courage. He has become a part of me in a strange and unexplained way. He talks about abiding in his friends. Such talk one cannot wholly understand, but the experience is very real, and infinitely satisfying."

"Do you think," asked Nicodemus, "that you could get from him a statement as to what his plans are? I asked you to come hither less to satisfy myself, than to seek some word that will satisfy the rulers. Some of them, as you know, are angered by what he has said and done, and some fear him. But there is none who is not impressed by his courage, and jealous of his power over the crowds. And we have always lived in hope that God will lay bare his arm in the sight of all people. There is always the chance that the messiah is in our midst, and that we see him not."

Thomas stood up excitedly and moved as if to take his leave.

"Perhaps," he said, "I can have from him such a word as you wish. I shall go at once to the Court of the Priests, and if I can, I shall return and bring you word. It may not be too late to avoid trouble."

The two men separated at the great portal of the house. It was a warm and cordial farewell Nicodemus spoke, and Thomas' heart was full of new eagerness and hope. He hurried toward the temple area, jostled by the crowds that filled the narrow streets, but he did not tarry until he had reached the Gate Beautiful. Here he stopped and reflected for a moment. Jesus was inside, thronged with a multitude that was listening in rapt attention to his words. It would be unwise to disturb the crowd with his question. Moreover, it was not such a question as could be put or answered in a word. That he fully knew. It were better to wait until he could talk without audience or interruption. Then he remembered that the disciples were to meet that evening in an upper room in a near-by street to partake together of the Passover feast. That would offer the best opportunity for his question. Thus decided, Thomas moved closer to the edge of the crowd that surrounded Jesus; and as he listened he felt once again the tug of that irresistible person, and the warm glow in his heart as he yielded once again to his persuasive and powerful words.

It was early twilight when they met for the feast. There was an anxiety that pervaded the room as distinct as the cooling air of the evening. Peter, the voluble, was boasting about his willingness to die in his friend's behalf. At the word "die," some of the others who had not thought of their danger in such terms, looked inquiringly at their friend.

"Let not your hearts be troubled," he said. "Trust in God: trust in me also . . . I am going to make ready a place for you . . . And where I am going, you all know the way."

A look of surprise swept over the faces dimly lit by the fresh tapers on the narrow table, when Thomas, who by reputation was the least talkative of the twelve, spoke up briskly and said:

"Master, we do *not* know where you are going. How should we know the way?"

Thomas was pleased to observe that several heads nodded assentingly. They waited for Jesus to speak.

"I am the way, the truth, and the life," he said quietly. "No man cometh unto the Father but by me."

Where Are You Going?

One's skepticism is, for the most part, one's own private affair. Endowed as man is with certain critical inclinations and faculties, he has a right to doubt everything from the deluge to the deity. Truth and error are empty of moral quality. There is no more reason to call a man wicked because he holds to an incorrect idea, than to discredit Stoicism because a Spartan lad once stole a fox.

Some people are born with a perverse spirit that excuses them for being normally suspicious, or incredulous, or inquisitive. There are periods in the life of all normal humans when skepticism is the prevailing mood. Adolescence is a time of philosophical disorder, induced by glandular changes. There are also times when one who customarily is phlegmatic, breaks out with a rash of doubt. Everything goes awry, and a mild epidemic seems to spread to all those who are in the neighborhood of the first victim. Such doubters are the result, less of some impulse or disorder within, than of some unaccustomed pressure or peril without. Once the turmoil subsides, doubt is relieved by a confidence that may be as jaunty as the doubt was dispiriting. And yet it is commonplace that nothing so quickly arouses distrust of a man's whole character as his expression of uncertainty about some great religious idea. He may question anything under the sun except a religious dogma and his reputation will suffer little, so long as he is not querulous or sullen; but the moment he hoists an interrogation point over what is called sacred truth, he is thought to have raised the distress signal of one already hopelessly sunk.

Thomas has had fastened upon him an odious nickname. Without any warrant from the scriptural record, he has been made Exhibit A of skepticism; and for centuries, an uncritical and unkind mind has neglected him in his unhappy historical niche. Had he been allowed to descend, to stretch himself and move about among common men, he would have long since appeared so wholly conventional that his title as patron saint of the skeptics would have given place to a distinction more exact and less invidious.

There is evidence to support the idea that Thomas was not a congenital dissenter. If, in a moment of tension, he refused to let a statement go unchallenged, it was not that he was a quarrelsome man. Nor have we good reason to think that his was a particularly critical intelligence. He is called the Doubter, but not to designate a brooding, studious sort of person. If there were such a man among the twelve, he was more likely to have been Nathanael, whose doubt that anything good could come out of Nazareth seems to have resulted from a long and careful study of Moses and the prophets. The silence of the record concerning Nathanael—he appears at only two points, and is thought to be Bartholomew at another—might be taken to indicate that there was little display of skepticism among the disciples, though such judgment may be hasty. In any case, the doubt of Thomas was so sudden and fleeting a thing that it should not have been allowed to establish his reputation.

Observe the places at which he appears in the record. For the major part of the ministry of Jesus he remained an inconspicuous member of the group. Scores of occasions had arisen in which a dissenter would have inevitably made himself heard from; but Thomas, if he doubted, ventured no comment. It is only as he is about to make his exit from the stage that his lines seem to betray his skeptic role. Once before this, however, his words and actions had given no hint of his sinister nature. On the contrary he steps up and confronts us as one, who in the face of a dangerous proposal, accepts its hazard boldly when it is evident that all but him were doubting its wisdom.

The Master had had trouble in Judea, his life had been threatened, and his disciples were glad to be quit of the place. There was little in retrospect to encourage their return. But word had come from Bethany that Lazarus was very sick, and Jesus decided finally to go to see him. The disciples undertook to dissuade him. "Lord, if he has fallen asleep, he will recover" (John 11:12). Observing their distress, he corrected his first report about Lazarus' condition. "Lazarus is dead," he said; and of course the quick retort was that that being the case, there was even less reason for risking the anger of the Judeans. One can, with little difficulty, imagine the eagerness with which the counsels of prudence were pressed on him by those whose dissent was compounded of doubt and fear. It was Thomas who broke the deadlock. Jesus' life had been threatened. Never mind that. The disciples shared his danger. Never mind that. "Let us go that we may die with him" (John 11:16). This heroic proposal may sound like resignation to inevitable fate, but by no sort of interpretation can it be made to represent the mind of a timid, equivocating, or skeptical man. In so far as heroism is almost always the active demonstration of great faith, Thomas showed nothing of the doubter there.

The last glimpse we have of him also fits poorly into the conventional picture of the man. He stands in a small group by the Sea of Galilee in the dawn, following the disruption of the fellowship by the death of the leader. With him were Peter, Nathanael, the two sons of Zebedee, and an anonymous pair. He has nothing to say, but his presence there is eloquent of a loyalty that had hitherto been rather spectacularly—and we have thought exclusively—demonstrated by Peter, James and John. In any case, there is nothing there pointing to his odious distinction as a doubter. One would more properly think that he gave evidence of a silent, stubborn fidelity that asked nothing except the privilege of being near his mysterious friend.

Between these two incidents in which calculating courage measured a risk and took it, and loyalty, strained and mystified, did not falter, occur two other glimpses of our man. The first, while the group was eating the paschal meal, presents him as replying to Jesus with an almost rude retort, repudiating the assumption the Master had made that his plans were clear to them all. So far as the record goes the rest of the crowd, no doubt as befogged as Thomas, said nothing. Thomas was honest, to the point of appearing almost abrupt. If he was skeptical, it commends him to us.

The second incident is the ground for his ill-repute. Unconvinced by the tales of excited women and the stories of the men, he declared his unwillingness to believe certain statements, which, unsupported by evidence, seemed fantastic. Those who believed Jesus alive had been convinced by what to them was proof. Thomas did not refuse to believe; he refused to believe without evidence. Here again his attitude commends itself to us; and if his skepticism was unworthy, then our whole modern structure of learning rests on a perverse and mischievous habit of mind.

We are allowed, then, to revise our estimate of this man, and to lift from him the odium he has so long carried. Had he been a suspicious or faithless man, we still would have to accord him the right to think as he pleased. But he seems to have been neither. A quiet, loyal, fearless friend, he found himself under the extreme pressure of uncertainty, protesting against an incorrect assumption; and when scolded by his fellows for being elsewhere than the upper room, he openly demanded proof for the incredible stories they told him.

Now we are able to see that Thomas, who shared the passion of his friend in a manner deeper, perhaps, than some of the others were able to, put, both for himself and all subsequent ages, the two most rudimentary questions that can be asked by religious faith in general, and Christian faith in particular. Indeed, his retort to Jesus is far more important than his retort to the disciples, for it supplies us not only with a true picture of Thomas, but frames for us the world's intermittent cry of bewilderment. Jesus had talked of going away, to a place, to prepare for their coming. And having said that, he added: "Whither I go, ye know; and the way ye know." Thomas replied: "Lord, we know not whither thou goest," and asked: "How can we know the way?" In the reply to Jesus, he raises the eternal difficulty about *ends*; and in the question, he raises the eternal difficulty about *means*. It was an inspired insight, growing out of the tension of the moment, and it puts on our own lips the deepest question of our own hearts. If we do not know *ends*, how can we know *means*? What was more important to Thomas? What is more important to us?

If we keep this in mind, we can understand more certainly the episode in the upper room ten days later. Thomas had posed a difficulty on Thursday night. The answer Jesus gave must have seemed to him, at the time, an impractical one. Certainly its meaning was less than complete in the trying hours during which he must have reflected on it. But when he confronted his friends that memorable evening, he perhaps still felt that the direction and the means Jesus had taken had fallen far short of achieving success. He had ignominiously died. What had *that* achieved? To Thomas death was no victory; it was terrible defeat. Little wonder he wanted evidence. Who, in his right mind, would have asked for anything else? But returning now to the more important word spoken to Jesus we are led to the judgment that Thomas, who for centuries has been accorded grudging sainthood, in spite of his alleged skepticism, deserves to be recanonized because of his courageous and discerning insight. Here was no man, disposed by his glandular organization to the reflective skepticism of a philosopher. Here was a man who, under the lash and spur of great emotional tension, responded not with mute assent or hysterical protest, but with a clear, profound and eternally relevant problem: We do not know where. How can we know how?

That Thomas' puzzled comment reflects the bewilderment of the ages can be seen at once by a glance at the history of the Christian movement. The way it has shifted direction and changed method is fairly staggering. This is what critics mean when they deplore what they call departures from the simple Galilean gospel. It is hardly an overstatement to say that so variously have the goals of Christianity been shifted about, and so devious have been the means employed in pursuit of these variable ends, that an account would include nearly everything that has happened in the Western world during the last nineteen centuries. No eddy in the stream of history, no idea in its library of thought, no room in its sprawling institutional structure lies outside the reach of Thomas' wisdom. Christianity has been a missionary movement, a political experiment, a romantic adventure,[1] and a military expedition as heartless and bloody as any tribal feud. It has provided excuse for the most obstinate obstruction of progress, credibility to the grossest superstition, and inspiration to the noblest exploits in human betterment. As it has changed its ends it has blessed them; as it has altered its means it has consecrated them. What other movement, in sober truth, is there in the history of the Western world that has both lifted and degraded mankind, exalted and despised human wisdom, corrupted and surfeited physical needs, and that has claimed all the while the holy radiance of Christianity as its guiding light? It has produced paupers and plutocrats, heretics and inquisitors, rebels and sycophants, saints and hypocrites, princes and slaves, despots and servants. It has raised its hands in prayer, and dipped them in blood; it has smitten humanity and bound up its wounds; it has furnished wisdom to children and withheld it from their fathers; it has flooded hearts with hope and drowned them in terror. And it is plausible to assume that never for a day during the flow of this majestic river of contradiction and power has the voice of Thomas been silent. Courageous, devout, loyal and hopeful, he has cried, "We do not know where you are going; how can we know the way?"

We make much in these studies of the anxiety that volatilized the atmosphere of Jesus' six last days, and have sought to explain some of the events of that short period within the framework of tension. Naturally, therefore, we feel that it was something in that tentativeness and vibration that gave vividness and focus to the misgivings that darkened the heart of this loyal and fearless friend. Had he been any less loyal, or any less fearless, he would hardly have risked, with his sharp retort, a rebuke from Jesus or the contempt of the disciples.

[1] Cf. the Arthurian legend of the 6th century as Tennyson recreates it:
". . . we strove in youth,
And brake the petty kings, and fought with Rome,
Or thrust the heathen from the Roman wall,
And shook him through the North."

Is it any wonder then, that once again, as we find ourselves living in times of great anxiety, greater perhaps than any period in history, we hear the cry of Thomas? Twenty-five years ago we thought we had found the way, and the means for reaching it. But that faith has defaulted, and that hope has vanished. If there be new goals and new ends it is not that they have been reasoned out by skeptics; they have been poured into hastily constructed molds from furnaces heated by the fires of fear or hatred.

It *is* the tension of our age that gives stridency to this cry and that amplifies its reverberations until its noise fills the heavens. Where are we going; and how shall we advance? And to this plea, the answers are forthcoming. H. G. Wells in his very newest book[2] replies: "Humanity which began in a cave, will end in the disease-soaked ruins of a slum." The salvation of man is "still just possible," however, and there follows a typical Wellsian program of redemption by education for democracy. Harry Elmer Barnes answers that the crisis in our civilization is coming so quickly (ten years or so), and that the alternatives are so staggering (utopia or barbarism), that there is no time for "pussyfooting and evasion." Vincent Sheean closes his new book thus:[3] "Upon the will and instinct of the proletariat reposes such hope as we are justified in retaining for the future progress of humanity through and beyond the conflict which now divides the world." Sir Arthur Salter outlines in his new book[4] a new proposal for security which he hopes may avert war and secure peace.

To the voice of these individual observers is added a babel of choruses that grow noisier every day. Where are we going? What is the way? Humanity is headed toward a classless society, and Marxism is the way. Mankind moves toward a super-state,

[2] H. G. Wells, *The Fate of Homo Sapiens* (Toronto: S. J. R. Saunders).

[3] Vincent Sheean, *Not Peace But a Sword* (New York: Doubleday, Doran & Company).

[4] J. A. Salter, *Security, Can We Retrieve It?* (New York: Reynal & Hitchcock).

and Fascism is the way. The Aryans are headed toward a super-race, and Blood and Soil is the way. Advices from the Orient repeat with significant emphasis the warning that the events that have so recently shattered the age-long calm of the East are not sporadic, unrelated incidents. They are parts of a plan carefully designed to bend the whole world to fealty to the Son of Heaven. Humanity, this seems to say, is headed toward one great Empire, and Shinto is the way.

The menace of these various claims lies in the fact that each uses the language of universal dominion. And well they may, for the essence of each is such as can brook no ultimate rivalry. For this reason we cannot laugh off the strut and bombast of their spokesmen. They may appear impostors or lunatics or clowns to us, but to themselves and their followers they are terrifyingly serious. And whatever we may think as to the time and role the cosmic stage will allow them, shout they will, and each will win his meed of hysterical and tempestuous applause, during his allotted hour.

In the light of this baleful comment, the relevance of Thomas' words for our day is inescapable. And it may be that many of us who confess preference for the claims of the Christian way over the ways of blood, soil, emperor and what not, will have to ask again, and seek an answer to Thomas' plaint. Whither are we bound? What has the Christian mind to say to that? And how are we to reach it?

This, of course, returns us to the record again, and to the reply that Jesus gave Thomas. The words are familiar. "I am the way . . . no man cometh unto the father but by me." If we reverse the order of the sentences we see that Jesus offered him a specific answer. In effect he said: mankind is moving in the direction of God. That is the *end* of humanity's pilgrimage. I am the way to reach God. That is the *means* of achievement. This is the language of Christian faith and aspiration; and however grievously the Christian movement may have sinned against it, it has always been ready to excuse its failures in the light of its hopes. But perhaps this familiar language is too familiar, familiar to the point of having dropped out of our range of conscious attention. We must therefore manage somehow to reassert it, if it is still valid and sufficient for the race.

For there are some who despair of the Christian goal, and some to whom the very words of Jesus are hateful. A certain contemporary historian characterizes Jesus' means for reaching God ("by means of me") as insufferable egotism. No spoken or implied claim by any other pretender to power can match that, he insists, for sheer spiritual arrogance. There is an answer to be made to that protest, though it lies outside the scope of our discussion. Our concern is with those who on the one hand are still hopeful that the Christian goal can be reached in the specified Christian way; and on the other hand with those who are less familiar with Christian words and phrases than they are with their own spiritual destitution and bewilderment. Such folk, and they are an innumerable host, will state their need not in the language of religion as such, but in the language of life. "What is it all about?" they ask, "and how are we to make our way?" Or perhaps they say: "We do not know where life is leading us, and how can we know the way?" Jesus told Thomas the goal was the Father, and the way was himself. Let us attend to the way John Macmurray summarizes it.[5] Humanity is headed toward communism, he says, but it is not the Russian sort. Rather is it a communism based on the ideal of the ancient Hebrew peoples: a beloved community in which man's ultimate loyalty is to God and the organization of society is in terms of justice, equality, and love. This is familiar ground. It is what we have known as the Kingdom of God. The interesting thing about such a statement is that a historian like Macmurray is compelled by the logic of events to return to the answer Jesus gave Thomas;

[5] John Macmurray, *The Clue to History* (New York: Harper & Brothers).

not exactly and in the same language, of course, but essentially and fundamentally the same idea.

There are many who will dispute this historian's prediction, not because they possess a more exact formula, but because they think man's concern with God is too largely spent to dominate life in the large. The point need not be argued here since its pros and cons are in the possession of all alert and inquiring minds. Let it be enough for the present intention to say that our world confusion comes about through the frantic pursuit by large segments of the human circle of mutually exclusive ends. As life becomes more complex and intimate, the points of friction multiply and the struggle to maintain one's end becomes increasingly difficult. The end of this is war. If there are not discovered a cohesive force and a single aim that transcend these lesser and contradicting goals, there is no prospect but that foreseen by H. G. Wells. No tendency of human movement that is away from a universal is either safe or continuous. For us, put in the language of Jesus, that means progress toward God.

Will Jesus be forced to yield to another as "the way," the means toward this ultimate end? Such a question does not disturb us when we discover that nearly every tendency in humanity takes its direction and finds its expression in persons of great power; that each colossus that strides the world is the enfleshment of an idea. The struggle in modern Germany is *Mein Kampf*, "my struggle." The confidence that all the world will some day come under the Son of Heaven is kept alive by the faith that the emperor *is* the Son of Heaven. For Jesus to say that it was by means of him that the advance of mankind was to be kept continuous and secure, was simply to use, in his day, language that has been understood in every age.

There are considerations other than the logic of events that compel our consent to the proposition that the only ultimate answer to the cry of Thomas is God and Christ. For us God is the end; for us Jesus is the means to that end. It is not enough that this has been true to the mind of many generations; nor is it enough that the experience of God in Christ has been reduced to rational statement by minds both exact and profound. The whole race of man must come to know it and experience it. How this is to be brought about is another matter. Mankind will learn partly through folly, and sin, and disillusionment, or even at last by some approximate chaos. And reflection, and simple ministry and worship will also add their persuasive testimonies. But this we fully believe, that when the stamping feet of the last pretender to human dominion are palsied by the touch of impartial and indifferent time, some later Thomas, still questing, and perhaps still harried by exigency will say: we do not know where you are going; and how shall we know the way? And the answer will come again, in a tongue alien to our own, no doubt, but spoken with a quiet confidence that will find response in every listening heart: "I am the way; no man cometh unto the Father but by me."

Chapter IV: PHILIP

Jew Meets Greek

Philip had recovered quickly from his surprise when Sosthenes accosted him in the Court of the Gentiles with the request to see Jesus, and had found himself greatly interested in the young Greek. Something in the directness of his speech and in the question he had posed, and, above all, in the manner in which Jesus seemed to respond to his words, impressed Philip. Sosthenes was forthright without being rude; he was young, and yet his thoughts seemed to reflect a mind both critical and mature.

Philip had secretly nurtured a strong admiration for the Greek world. Born in Bethsaida of Galilee, a spot that had grown from a small fishing village to a busy and beautiful town under Philip the Tetrarch, he had been given his Greek name by a mother whose pride in her city was recognized by calling her son by the name of its builder. The three-century-old defeat of Greece by Rome had not dimmed, in Philip's estimate, the luster of the great King of Macedon who had given his name its original glory; and often as a lad at play, he had imagined himself as Philip the Great, and the fishing boat of his father as the royal trireme. Within the Galilean fellowship, he was one of the few who bore a Greek name; and when several of the others won from Jesus Greek sobriquets, it was to Philip's unconfessed satisfaction a somewhat belated though genuine admission of the superiority of the renown of Greece over the melancholy annals of his own people.

For this reason, Philip determined to seek an opportunity for further conversation with the visitor, but it was not until early Thursday morning that the chance occurred. He had

come into the city after spending the night beyond the Kidron.
It had been a time of scant rest, for the disciples had been
disputatious and even quarrelsome far into the night. The
Master had sought to check their petulance by words of promise; but they seemed to forget his assurance of victory to those
who held out to the end, because of his predictions of wars
and disturbances, so soon to come to pass. And just before
midnight, Judas of Kerioth had departed suddenly from the
group, refusing to respond to Jesus' call as he made off into
the dark.

Philip was reflecting on these circumstances while he ate a
meager breakfast at a stall near the south gate, and when,
moving at length into the temple area he spied the four
Greeks sitting again by the balustrade where two days before
he had seen them the first time, he walked briskly up to them,
and saluted cordially. They rose to acknowledge his nod.
Recognition was mutual and the returned greeting was
friendly.

"I speak you peace," said Philip.

"May the God of Israel bless you and keep you," the men
replied.

Philip's eye rested for an instant on the notice cut in the
stone balustrade, as he moved to accept a seat offered him beside Sosthenes.

"And was the night spent in quietness and rest?"

"Nay, rather, in quarreling that banished sleep until three
hours before the dawn," Philip answered, dolefully.

"And pray, what cause should disturb your friends, that
they cannot rest. There was great beauty in the moonlit evening for us, and the coolness of the night air above these hills
was balm for weariness." The three other men nodded their
agreement.

"Perhaps," said Philip, "we are overborne. Since leaving
Galilee there has been little time for repose. The Master knows
neither weariness nor rest so long as there is need for ministry

of word or gentleness. But some of the group are restless and unhappy. For all these months we have rejoiced to share with him long days of labor among the simple folk of village and countryside. But here in the great city we seem to have lost our way. There is less time for listening to him, and more for making holiday. These pilgrims listen for a moment, and then go on their way to the pleasure booths along the wall. It is not like the long, happy hours by roadside or inn . . ."

"Does he himself plan to do more than to celebrate the Passover?" It was Sosthenes who interrupted. "Will he worship, and then return to his works of mercy in Galilee, or do you think he is set upon a mighty demonstration of the power of God, before this great festival multitude?"

"I do not know. Last night Judas of Kerioth left us, angered, I thought, by something Jesus had said to him. I did not hear what he said, but as Judas left he flung back a heated word about the need, at last, for ending his eternal chatter about love, and doing something practical to impress the crowds."

"Sharp words," observed Sosthenes, "spoken by one who apparently has lost his grip on himself. And yet there may be a measure of truth in what he said."

Philip did not reply, but his gaze was fixed on the young man as if he were hopeful that he would go on. But for a moment Sosthenes kept silent. Philip's eyes wandered and rested again for a shame-filled moment upon the hateful warning on the balustrade. He was on the point of apologizing for the words when Sosthenes began talking quietly again.

"I have been interested to compare," he said, "the Greek and the Roman and the Hebrew religious minds. I was taught in my small school in Corinth that the decline of the Greek people came about less through the power of Rome than through the impractical nature of Greek culture. This may be simply an easy way of excusing ourselves, but . . ."

"The Great Alexander was a Greek," put in one of Sosthenes' companions, "and he was a practical man."

"True, yet less a Greek than a Macedonian, and less a Macedonian than a man," countered Sosthenes, laughing.

"What I mean is that Greek culture was primarily aesthetic. It was art, and philosophy, neither of which, one must admit in our practical day, seems to have much practical value. Greek religion also, such as it was, and where it differed from philosophy, was largely stories about impossible and impractical creatures who were called gods, but who acted in very strange, not to say quite human ways."

"Like angels?" asked Philip.

"Perhaps," said Sosthenes. "But the similarity between Greek and Hebrew religious ideas is closer than that. While the commandment against images has helped to keep religion a spiritual experience here, it has also tended to keep it unrelated to actual life. It is the Roman who has hit upon the practical way. Rome has encouraged all sorts of religious ideas and permits all varieties of religious images. But it sees to it that Caesar is put at the center of the religious life of the Roman. He is god to them, and he is a very practical sort of man—or god, after all."

"And would you remove the ban on images?" asked Philip incredulously. "And should we worship Caesar as our god? Such words are indeed ill-spoken in these precincts." There was a note of annoyance in his voice.

"No, not at all," Sosthenes answered, as if unmindful of Philip's anxious tone. "There is nothing but evil in the worship of images; and to worship any man is to dilute religion to admiration, or degrade it to fear. But if somehow through the Hebrew people who have clung to the spiritual nature of religion, God could be made visible again . . ."

"Moses saw him in a burning bush . . ." interrupted Philip.

"Yes, and became a great leader in a time of crisis."

"And Isaiah saw him in the smoke of altar incense . . ."

"Yes," responded Sosthenes eagerly, "and he too became a

great leader in a critical time. So also Jeremiah, and Daniel . . ."

"What do you think would happen," Philip interposed, "if the Master could give a vision of the Father to this multitude of Passover worshipers?"

"What would happen?" echoed Sosthenes. "History gives you your answer. In every age of crisis it is the man who makes God evident to practical people, meeting practical needs, who wins a following. Did not Alexander call himself a god, and conquer the world?"

That evening, as the members of the little group reclined on their couches in an upper room and listened as Jesus talked to them, Philip was very quiet. So quiet indeed was he, that he appeared to be listless or inattentive. For nearly an hour the Master had been talking. His words had soothed and sweetened the spirits of his friends, friends who during the hours previous to the supper had been ill-tempered and almost unruly. He was speaking of going away and intimated that they would shortly follow him. Philip vaguely thought that he meant his return to Galilee after the festival; but Thomas, to the surprise of all, blurted out sharply,

"We do not know where you are going, and how can we know the way?"

There was an embarrassed pause. All eyes turned toward Thomas, who was discomfited by the interruption he had caused. Then Jesus, without raising his voice, spoke to Thomas.

Philip, brought suddenly back from his mental wanderings by the retort of Thomas waited until Jesus had finished; and then, to the astonishment of all, spoke up with a tone of voice that sounded as impatient as a command.

"Lord, show us the Father and we will be satisfied."

The twelve looked at each other with expressions of amused and then of resentful bewilderment. It was clear that this irrelevant intrusion had, for the moment, broken the spell of the Master's restful discourse. Yet he alone of the group was unperturbed by the unexpected demand. He turned to Philip and said confidently:

"Have I been with you so long a time, Philip, and do you not yet know me? He that hath seen me hath seen the Father. How sayest thou then 'show us the Father'?"

SHOW US GOD

Little wonder that Philip never wrote a gospel. Not even the writers of apocryphal records thought of using his name or reputation pseudonymously. The late Dr. David Smith disposed of him as a dull, superficial man. It cannot truly be said that there are no books written by dull, superficial men; but it is true that the Gospels were written by quite another sort. It may be, after all, to his credit that he refused to yield to the literary urge.

Withal, however, he is an interesting man, even if Dr. Smith has rightly judged him. Superficiality may be a device that dullness wears to compensate or protect itself, but it is often a gay garment. And if we run through the appearances of this man on the stage of the gospel drama, we may find him momentarily interesting, or significant, or even important.

He confronts us first as he responded immediately to an invitation given him by Jesus, who was about to return to Galilee. He is identified in the story as a friend and fellow townsman of Peter and Andrew. They may have been his sponsors, since their credentials were somewhat detailed; Philip, on the contrary, is presented without specified credits. His sudden excitement at being invited to join the little group sent him dashing off to share the news of his good fortune with one who seems to have been an old friend—Nathanael. It is unlikely that Philip had had time to reflect on the meaning of this young Galilean carpenter for the destiny of the nation;

but according to the record, he had sized him up with a glance as the fruition of the hopes of Israel. This might be construed as insight, almost as clairvoyance indeed, had it not been that another remark rather gives him away. Nathanael appears to have been a brooding, melancholy man whose long study of the lore of his people and whose survey of the contemporary scene had left a deposit of solid and uncomfortable despair in his soul. The quick enthusiasm of Philip woke no bird to sing in the dark wood of his pessimism. With something akin to exasperation he protested to Philip in a word that was both a rebuke to his informer and a confession of his own distrust. "Can anything good come out of Nazareth? You ought to know better than that." For in support of his contention that Jesus was the fulfillment of the writings of Moses and the prophets, Philip had offered the most inadequate support. "He is Jesus, Son of Joseph, who comes from Nazareth." Certainly a messiah needed more than name and address as surety.

Nor was Philip's rejoinder conspicuously profound. Instead of defending his amazing claim, he glibly passed the obligation of proof over to Nathanael. He was sure of the Messiah's name, family and town, but nothing more. In response to the demand for further evidence he replied, "Come and see," in other words, prove it for yourself. It needs hardly to be said that had Jesus' claims to Messiahship rested on no more impressive data than that supplied by Philip, he might as well have spent the rest of his life in Nazareth. Philip's enthusiasm was a poor substitute for the evidence needed to convince a man like Nathanael. Superficial, is Dr. Smith's word, and we cannot disagree.

But dull? Here we may be allowed to demur for reasons more convincing even than the obvious fact that enthusiasm is itself rarely dull. For Philip exhibits a quality that modifies in an important way his reputation for dullness. He was a very practical man; realist is what his like is called today. Indeed it may

have been his eye for practical values that made him quick to
try anyone who might possibly turn out to have the qualities
desired and needed in a national leader. He was willing to
let Nathanael scrutinize the law and the prophets for clues;
he, however, insisted on scouting around the country for a person. His impatience with books was corollary to his enthusiasm
for taking chances.

This quality finds expression in another picture we have
of him. The scene was the famous one on the hill near Jerusalem, just before one of the Passover festivals. The pilgrims
crowding the road to the city were hungry and tired at the end
of the day, and their plight laid its demands on Jesus. Resolved to feed them, he turned to Philip and asked: "Where
shall we buy bread for all these people to eat?" The record
comments editorially that this was to put Philip to the test
since Jesus knew what he was going to do.

Philip met the test as a practical man. One less matter-of-
fact might have suggested that manna be catered by heaven.
A proposal had once been made to Jesus to turn stones into
bread, for a quite practical use. But if Philip's mind was
seduced by such fancies there is no evidence of it. On the
contrary he seems to have looked at the multitude, made a
lightning calculation and reported his judgment in figures.
Name and address; dollars and cents; that is the practical man's
way. He stopped, closed his eyes and counted: "Fourteen
hundred six-pence loaves; each person half a loaf, twenty-eight
hundred half loaves—" He opened his eyes and looked at the
crowd again. "No," he replied confidently. "Seven pounds'
worth of bread" (Weymouth's translation), replied Philip,
"is not enough for them to get even a scanty meal." Practical,
but hardly dull.

To one concerned with practical matters, Philip's famous
request of Jesus was very much to the point. For three years,
Jesus had conducted with his friends a laboratory experiment

in righteous living. It was different from the righteousness of the Pharisees which, because formalized and stereotyped, was impractical. As they had come this year to Jerusalem for the holiday season, they were confronted with practical difficulties that were not likely to be overcome by anything short of practical methods. It was to be expected then, that as the group met in the upper room there should have been a feeling on the part of some that they must come to grips with the situation. Judas was bent on a practical and desperate course. Jesus talked about going away to prepare a place for them. But he seemed proposing to leave them until he could come for them. Leave them in the midst of uncertainty and possible danger? That was most impracticable!

It may be that the unexpected retort of Thomas and its tone of bewilderment gave Philip the needed urge. Thomas was distressed. So were they all. But the confusion might possibly be cleared up so that the Master would not need to go away, and their tarrying in Jerusalem would present no needless hazard. What to the devout and God-fearing mind could be more convincing than a sight of God? If, in response to the prayer of Jesus, God could be seen by the twelve, they would be satisfied, the perplexity Thomas had voiced would vanish, and—if perchance that beatific vision could be seen by the multitudes, the problems of the fellowship would disappear, and the success of the movement would be assured. It was Philip, superficial, we admit, but not dull, who asked for a practical solution. "Show us the Father, and we will be satisfied."

Philip may have never risen any higher than that, but considering the man, that was fairly high. It would not have been inconsistent with our picture of him if he had proposed, on the spot, a dissolution of the fellowship before it proved too late. It lifts him in our estimation when he appears trying to make a practical approach to the center of man's ultimate concern.

In this stern hour when the spirit falters
Before the weight of fear, the nameless dread;
When lights burn low upon accustomed altars
And meaningless are half the prayers we've said—
Faith seeks a rock, immovable, unchanging,
On which to build the fortress of its strength;
Some pole-star, fixed, beyond the planets' ranging
Steadfast and true throughout the journey's length.[1]

This was what Philip wanted, a fact big enough, a confidence firmly established, "immovable, unchanging . . . steadfast and sure." He thought the sight of God would answer that need.

And yet in the way in which Philip hoped for it, it was an impossible request. And for this reason it lays bare an error that many make who think themselves practical. From this also it follows, that some of the difficulty that men in our modern age have with God lies just here.

The delight that all of us have with practical matters, the use and handling of practical things, inevitably makes us uninterested in, or distrustful of things that cannot be brought within reach of our five senses. Before men in the mass could clock speed on a dial, weigh values on a scale, extract truth with an equation, they accepted many things as true solely on the word of other similarly credulous souls. No little that they accepted was nonsense, but it was believed in with no less ardor than the most irrefutable fact. It is simply a part of the dialectical process, that finally having had instruments of precision put in his hands, man's mind should have swept out into the cold wastes of agnosticism concerning ideas his hands could not touch. Most people prefer a limited power they can see, to an infinite power they cannot see. They would rather worship a golden calf than an invisible deity above the sum-

[1] Josephine Johnson: *Harpers Magazine.*

mit of Sinai. Every once in so often we agree that we live by what we call imponderables—faith, hope, and love; but we are careful that we shall have tangible or visible proof of their reality. Since the very word imponderable suggests they cannot be measured on balances, we supply this defect by using symbols that *can* be weighed. There will come a time, and of its return we are confident, when the swing of faith toward measurable things will feel the pull again that will restore faith in things that being invisible are also eternal.

But what Philip wanted was impossible, and will, we think, always be. What he wanted, to judge by Jesus' reply, was no showing forth of God in metaphysical terms. The mind of Philip is manifestly typical of the mind of the race in this regard. He could not have understood or acknowledged a complete demonstration of God in terms of logic or philosophy. The wisest of men have never been able to do much more, by rational processes, than move around the circumference of the idea. If they have plunged into its center and come forth with a radiant consciousness of God, their experience was irrational; they have had a "seventh heaven" experience like Paul; theirs is the mystic's rapturous beholding. The wisest of men cannot excogitate God. We speak no irreverent word when we say that the possibility was similarly beyond the reach of Jesus.

Moreover, to have answered the request would have involved one or the other of two things. Either it would have been necessary to shrink God to such dimensions as are comprehensible by the mind of men; or the mind of Philip would have needed expanding to such vast size that he could have comprehended the infinite. The first process would have reduced God to humanity; the second would have elevated Philip to deity. And this is the danger that is always encountered by those who seek to answer for themselves the demand Philip made of Jesus. Since God to be recognized would have to present himself in a form suggesting the human, God would tend to be humanized; since to see the invisible is to possess super-human faculties, man would tend to self-deification. Either one is fatal to the authentic religious experience, for the first ends in atheism, and the second in egoism.

Aside from these difficulties, the more practical one arises as to whether even in the event that the request could have been met, it would have satisfied Philip, the practical man. There would have been a moment of shock perhaps, and then of ecstasy, as when one who believes vaguely in beauty confronts a great painting, hears a great symphony, reads a great line of poetry, or stands for a breathless moment before the red resurgence of the day. But after the surprise and delight, the spirit would have subsided to its accustomed level again. This was, in Philip's mind, the same vague hope that constituted the second temptation of Jesus. When he was urged by that plausible voice to throw himself down from the temple, he heard the same word Philip spoke, except that Philip wanted to see God, and Jesus was being urged to show God's auxiliaries at work. The angels would not let his feet be dashed against the stone. But Jesus knew then as he knew when Philip tempted him, that one leap would call for another; and a spiritual ministry would be reduced to acrobatics to amuse the crowds. The moment the leaping stopped the crowd was sure to go away; and if it kept up for any considerable time, the crowd would grow tired and demand higher and more hazardous leaps. No, Philip would not have been satisfied with the sight of the Father. He would have remembered his experience for a while, but being a practical man, he would have soon felt a need for another proof, bigger and better than the last.

This is eminently characteristic of the practical person. His satisfactions lie less in seeing and holding, than in advancing from one thing to another. No less than the philosopher the empiricist is never wholly satisfied, and such satisfaction as he wins is less in acquisition than in quest.[2] Is not this true of the scientist? Twenty-five hundred years ago on a guess by a Greek, men started looking for the atom. They were finally "shown" the atom, but it did not satisfy them. Since then they have sought and found the electron and the proton, and now, less satisfied than Anaxagoras was with his atom, they are bombarding the proton that they may see what it is that holds the physical universe together. From organ to tissue, from tissue to cell, from cell to nucleus, from nucleus to chromosome, from chromosome to enzyme the quest goes on in the organic realm. When man was recently announced to be "only a colloidal oxynitrocarbide of hydrogen with some admixture, chemically speaking," it satisfied very few practical people. In the light of this questing spirit of man it is not implausible for us to imagine Philip, after gazing in astonishment at God for a while, regaining practical interest enough to look behind the blaze of glory to see what was back of the Absolute!

> One prayed a sight of heaven; and erewhile
> He saw a workman at his noontime rest.
> He saw one dare for honor, and the smile
> Of one who held a babe upon her breast;
> At dusk two lovers walking hand in hand,
> But did not understand.[3]

No, it would not have satisfied; and yet we share, more or less, his wish. Lloyd George promised the new recruits in England in 1914 a world fit for heroes when they returned victorious. But a world fit for heroes—meaning a world with no battles to fight—would produce no heroism, and heroes would find it intolerable. A world fit for philosophers—meaning a world

[2] The childhood ambition of Ida M. Tarbell was to be a biologist and own a microscope, through the eyes of which she hoped to rediscover God. Instead she became a writer. It is likely her discovery of God was not confused by the change!

[3] Victor Starbuck, "The Seekers," *The World's Great Religious Poetry*: Hill-Macmillan.

where all the questions are answered—would turn out, after all, to be a pedant's world, where little folk would be unhappy, having no queries to baffle their elders with. By the same token a world in which God could be seen would not necessarily be a world in which God would be adored. It might, on the contrary, be a world where he was ignored. And yet that "never ending, never sated search for God" as Gamaliel Bradford put it, seems integral to the religious experience. Is not this the "mystery of godliness"?

From what has been said it is obvious that we have been evading Philip's question, we who live in an age boastful of its pragmatic mind, where mental speculation is distrusted to such an extreme that some have had to cry out against the cults of anti-rationalism and the deliberate low-brow. Do we not give religion the slip when we say it does not need to be realistic? Quite, but the point of this is that to be practical is not always to be realistic, and vice versa. We have long consented to the idea that Jesus was one of the most realistic of men. Was he always the most practical? Right now there are those who attest to the burning realism of the insight of Jesus into life and destiny who demur when asked to agree that his way of enhancing life's beauties and repairing its sin is practical. He saw that anger was more terrible than murder because it was the parent of the overt act; but when he said that the way to deal with evil was to turn the other cheek, we repudiate angrily the notion that such folly can bring practical results in overcoming evil.

This brings us to the reply that Jesus made to his inquisitor, for he did not argue nor evade. With a realism as disarming as it was practical he replied—and with a lift of surprise inflecting his words: "Have I been so long with you, and have you not known me, Philip? He that has seen me has seen the Father; how then can you say; show us the Father?"

This clearly says that such glimpses of the Father as we are to be allowed will not come in a unique, spectacular or bizarre way. God is revealed to us in the obvious. "Have not I been here so long?"

> Whether you go to tome or star,
> You dig too deep, you soar too far,
> My friend! Some day when winter's gone,
> Go lie full length upon the lawn
> And watch the tides of life that pass
> Among the slim stems of the grass.
> . . . .
> The stars are far. Lie on the sod
> 'And let your spirit soak up God![4]

This is poetry, but not for that reason, impractical. It is the familiar language of religion too. The mystical experience of being filled with the divine spirit is perhaps the private secret of the possessor, but its reality is attested to by common-place acts that betray the divine presence in the heart of the actor. If we have not eyes to see God in the obvious, how shall we see him in the enigmatical? And if, after "so long" being with Jesus, Philip had not seen the lineaments of God, was he likely to see them better—or for more practical use—in a blinding and transient vision?

But this says something else too. It is in him, we see God, not in everything that is obvious. The problem of evil would have found no solution in a vision of God, but the assurance of good would have been fortified. And was that not implicit in what Jesus said? God is to be seen in the best we see. Wherever redemption is at work—and the word must be extended to its widest limits—there is God. This answers no question about the fact of evil. If Philip had said, "Show us the meaning of evil and we will be satisfied," his proposition would have been more to our liking perhaps. But that aspect of the problem must wait for an answer.[5] Speaking of God as an ex-

[4] From "The Philosopher of Folly," *Cleveland Plain Dealer*.

[5] Chapter IX, *The Social Manifesto of Jesus* (New York: Harper & Brothers). The author's effort to suggest an answer.

perience of the "inner life of the soul," Auguste Sabatier wrote many years ago: "I may disdain the inner life of the soul, and divert myself from it by the distractions of science, art, and the social life; but if wearied by the world of pleasure or of toil, I wish to find my soul again and live a deeper (God illumined) life, I can accept no other guide and master than Jesus Christ, because in him alone is optimism without frivolity, and seriousness without despair." That satisfied Sabatier. After all, the reason Jesus has been invested with divinity is not because those who saw him made appropriate and accurate metaphysical deductions about his nature. It was rather because by his hands God unerringly wrought his ministries of love, and through his face the light of God undiminishably gleamed.

It remains to say that as in the other studies the fact of tension has contributed much to what was said and done, so we see in this episode the pressure of an extreme need making itself felt. Was it not the pall of uncertainty that shrouded Philip's mind that made him cry for a shaft of ethereal glory that would pierce the darkness and show God to him? And was there not the feeling that such a vision, if generally and widely granted, would make their way safer and more successful?

And once again we sense the tension of our day that is inspiring in practical hearts a cry for the sight of God, and the hope that such a sight might bring sanity and security to a shaken world. Everything we hold dear—democracy, the inviolability of covenants, the right to work and a measure of economic security and happiness, even the culture of the ages—these all seem precariously held in feeble hands, and threatened by the swinging fists of egotists and megalomaniacs. Show us a new alliance, a new axis, a new balance of power, a new source of wealth, a new protection against danger! Show

us God, and it will satisfy us! It is in such times of pressure
that practical men cry out often for impractical expedients
to save them. Do we want to see God standing like the Olym-
pian Jove, hurling thunderbolts, or like the ancient wall of
fire standing between us and the advance of our enemies? Do
we want to see him as protector or as judge, destroying our
enemies or condemning our sin? Or do we want to see him
at all; or do we dare? Suppose, for the moment, that such a
wish could be humored, and our yearning for certitude grati-
fied by a vision of God, obvious and unmistakable. This circumstance has been imagined by a poet whose work is little
known, but whose insight is authentic. In a poem entitled
"The Lifting of the Veil"[6] he pictures what took place one day
when the mantle that covers the face of God was drawn, and
the world of men stopped, stark and stricken at the sight.

> The Veil was lifted
> And the Face was there!
> The heart of the city
> Stood silently;
> How could they barter,
> How could they traffic
> With the terrible Eyes to see?
> Nay! Each man brooded
> On the Face alone;
> Each soul was an Eyeball,
> Each shape was a stone;
> And I saw the faces,
> And some were glad,
> And some were pensive,
> And some were mad;
> But in all places,
> Hall, street and lane—
> 'Twas a frozen pleasure
> A frozen pain.

The fact is that absolute sight in such matters, whether

[6] *The Book of Orm*, by Robert Buchanan.

real or imagined, is a sort of spiritual paralysis. He who boasts that he apprehends the ultimate has only lost sensation; he mistakes numbness for certainty. The dimming of the light that would blind us if its full blaze fell upon our unprotected eyes is God's appointment in the region of the infinite.

This is peculiarly interesting in the light of a recurrent interest in theology—or more properly a concern with God. This has come about by default. After two or three decades, disillusionment with scientific humanism is fairly complete. Its faith: put your trust in science and have confidence in yourself, was overcome by a curious mischance. The scientific analysis of man left him little to feel confident about. Show us man and it sufficeth us, was the cry. And a vision was supplied in terms of iron, sugar, lime, phosphorus, magnesium, potassium, and sulphur, and it failed, somehow, to satisfy.

And we must be careful lest this new practical interest in God be deflected into the quest for practical certainty such as Philip sought. We ought to know better now; but if we are not sufficiently warned by Philip's error, perhaps the caution suggested by one whose major interest is physics instead of theology, will help. "Systematic investigation of matter and energy without regard for immediate *practical* (italics mine) ends has turned out to be the most direct road to social riches . . . Practicality is inevitably short-sighted, and is self-handicapped by the fact that it is looking so hard for some single objective that it may miss much that nature presents."[7]

Somehow we seem to return to an earlier day that was troubled in much the same way as our own and hear above the din of our own voices an ancient word: "He that has seen me has seen the Father." Do I want to see God? Look at Jesus. To know how he acts? Watch Jesus. And to know what God wants of me? Listen to Jesus. That is not the end of our quest; it is the beginning. It will not satisfy as an ultimate fact, but it will satisfy us as the ultimate experience.

[7] George Russell Harrison, *Atoms in Action* (New York: William Morrow and Co.).

Chapter V: JAMES AND JOHN

The Feast Is Prepared

Early in the afternoon of Thursday, Salome, wife of Zebedee and mother of James and John, raised herself on her couch, and listened to what she thought was a rap on the outer door. She had been resting during the hot two-hour period that stifled the crowded city as the sun began its slow descent from the meridian; and her room, carefully shuttered against the glare, had been both quiet and cool. The rap was repeated outside, impatiently. She slipped her feet into her sandals and was on the point of answering the summons when she heard the shuffling feet of a servant girl crossing the court. Moving to the window, she swung the heavy wooden shutter half open and looked out into the white sunlight. As the outer portal creaked open, a tall man, his head protected against the heat by a looping fold of his tunic, entered the yard. He balanced a large water jar on one shoulder, and as he stooped slightly to avoid the low lintel, a few drops of the water spilled, and spattered in a silver cascade over the servant girl. The water carrier laughed as he set the jar down, quite undisturbed by the sharp words of the young woman who, flicking uselessly at the dark spots that mottled her robe, turned to the gate again, and closed it.

She did not slip the wooden bolt into the socket. The moment the door swung to, a sharp knock and the noise of voices stopped her. She opened the gate slightly again, and looking suspiciously through the narrow crack, saw two men.

"We were told," said one of them, somewhat out of breath, "to follow the man with the water jar, and to ask the master of the house . . ."

"The master is not in," the maid replied curtly.

"To ask the master," the man went on, "where the room is, in which we are to prepare the Passover."

She scrutinized the faces of the men for a moment, and then slowly drew the gate open again, wide enough to allow their entrance.

"Come in," she invited; "you are from Galilee?"

"Yes," they answered, and stepped quickly inside. The maid slipped the bar noiselessly into place and started toward the house.

Through the half-opened shutter, Salome had seen her two sons step inside the gate, and was waiting at the low door of the house when they reached it. She touched her lips with her finger, to warn them lest their surprise at seeing her there betray them into noisy talk.

"The mother of the Teacher is sleeping in there," she said. "We must not disturb her. She has been very tired, and sleeps fitfully. Come into my room." She led them back to her cool chamber, and bade them sit on the long couch near the window.

"We did not know you were here," John said mysteriously. "He said nothing of Mary's being here either. Only the command to follow the man with the water jar. Is it here that we shall eat the feast?"

"Yes, and it is nearly prepared. All that lacks is getting the food. The room is ready; it is a large and comfortable place." She raised her eyes and pointed to the ceiling as she spoke. "An upper room, where you can sup in quietness and in safety."

"You say his mother rests not well?" asked James solicitously.

"Nay, she scarcely sleeps at all," replied Salome. "Since Monday she has been afraid. Last night at midnight, she cried out, and when I went into her room she was sitting up, her hands gripped tightly over her heart, and a look of terror in her eyes. 'A pain, like to the sharp thrust of a sword, racks me here,' she said. I gave her a breath of camphor leaves to smell, and she was quieted at length."

"Yes," said James, "we are all of us afraid, all except him. If he is afraid, he betrays it by no word or sign. Perhaps when she awakes, we can tell her not to fear since he is unafraid. Or when he comes tonight, he can comfort her. That were better."

"Tell me," Salome demanded gently of them, "what is he going to do?"

"After the supper tonight, he will return to the Garden of Olives," answered John.

"Can he not stay here; is it not safer here than there?"

"To one who has no fear, one place is as safe as another," laughed James.

"But, I was thinking not of tonight," corrected Salome, "but of—well, of the years ahead. Those who are his followers expect so much of him; and they that hate and fear him—they will surely not suffer him forever. Monday morning in the temple . . ."

"I think," interrupted John, "he wishes that had not happened."

"Perhaps," countered his mother, "but it did happen; and it drove a wedge between his friends and his enemies. His mother is full of misgivings. She would have him return with her to Nazareth. I—I would see him seize the power that waits but for his grasp . . ."

"Nay, good mother," warned James. "Do you forget his word to you when you sought positions for us on his left and right when he was to grasp—as you put it now—his Kingdom?"

"I forget nothing," she answered animatedly. "He promised you a cup to drink and a baptism to undergo. Did that not mean that after your cup was drained, you would be rewarded?"

"I think it was not thus that he intended," John answered. "He promised us nothing. He reminded us that rewards and positions and such like were not his to give."

"So you have not urged him to seize power, and promised your support to him?" asked Salome. "And is there still bitterness to drain from new cups; and must this baptism of his engulf us all, his weary mother and me and . . . ?"

James took the hand that had been stressing her fretful words with brisk, impatient gestures, and his touch quieted her.

"You are the mother of the sons of thunder," he said smiling. He looked at his brother and continued: "It is hard to know sometimes the source of the clouds and the lightnings, and the winds that ruffle the waters of the lake. But here . . ."

John nodded and laughed understandingly, and took hold of her other hand, lifting her gently to her feet. He slipped his arm about her, and let her head rest on his ample shoulder. She understood the rebuke, and was quiet for a moment. Presently she looked up into the face of her strong son and said:

"But if it is not to be brought about thus, how can his mother's puzzled heart be set at peace?"

"I do not know," John answered wearily. "I asked him once about his home in Nazareth, and he spoke that strange word about leaving father and mother and houses and lands for the sake of the gospel. I do not think he will abandon us to danger, but I do not think he will endanger the gospel by seizing power. We have talked much with him of late. He talks of wars and rumors of wars, of broken homes and divided families, of friends who prove false, and of faithfulness to the end."

"And yet he will not stop it with a sign, or avert it by proclaiming himself as King? There is nothing he cannot do . . ."

"Nothing, indeed, except those things which his love forbids. There is much I do not understand; but this I know: he will not fight for power."

Salome looked from one face to the other. Both men seemed slightly stooped with weariness, and the lines about their faces indicated that they had been keeping long and sleepless vigils in their meeting place under the olive trees. And for the moment her vigorous and anxious mind was quieted by tenderness and solicitude, and she searched her heart for some intimation of ministry she might bring to her sons. At length she said, as if her concern for Jesus were quite forgotten:

"Will you not rest here for an hour? There is time, and it is quiet; and sleep will refresh your bodies. I will fetch water that you may bathe your faces. Have off your sandals, let me wash your feet."

She pushed them gently down on the divan, and they submitted to her attentions by kicking off their sandals and rolling back their sleeves. As Salome stooped to pick up an earthen basin, she heard a sound in the door, and turning, saw Mary the mother of Jesus standing, framed by its rough outlines. Her eyes, somber and dark with weariness and the intuitions of tragedy, lighted for a moment as she recognized the two men; and her greeting though cursory was cordial.

"The feast," she said, looking toward Salome who had not risen from her bending posture, "the feast. Must we not put it in readiness? He will be here at the set of sun, and wishes not to be delayed. He says that he will have other business after supper, beyond the brook. He will meet someone in the garden. I hope it is a friend."

"Yes," the other woman said, indulgently, "there is but little to be done. I have already arranged the couches, and the boys will presently go out to buy some wine."

She stood up and moved toward the door. "There is a jar of water freshly brought. It is cool. Will you not also be refreshed by it?"

"Nay," said Mary, "it is my heart that is weary, and what water—what water—" She stopped as though challenged by a recollection—"what water can refresh the heart?"

She turned and disappeared into the shadows. In a moment more there were sounds as of someone stirring in the room above. James and John looked at the ceiling and then at each other, but did not speak.

TIRED RADICALS

The most famous triumvirate in history is not Caesar, Pompey, and Crassus—statesman, soldier, and politician—but Peter, James, and John—three fishermen. If celebrity has a statistical basis in the number of those who know a fact or a name, it is perhaps true to say that these three Galileans have been known to as many millions as the three Romans have been known to thousands. If, however, fame is a matter of the achievement of some monumental benefit or villainy, the award might still go to the fishermen, for the influence of their acts persists strangely to this hour. The venal and corrupt politicos of the modern age do not invoke the shades of Crassus; but the prayers of millions still implore the mediations of St. Peter, St. James and St. John.

Our present study is concerned with the latter two of this famous trio, but not in any way that dissociates them from Peter. He is to be the subject of a chapter that will follow, and yet it is impossible to lift him entirely out of this charmed association. But James and John were brothers, and if our guidance in such matters is trustworthy, they were blood-cousins of Jesus, their mother Salome having been a sister of the mother of the Lord. Peter's kindred were obscurer folk, save for his brother Andrew and his father John, who lived in the fishing quarter of the lakeside town Capernaum. Whether or not this blood-relation made for a closer bond between Jesus and his cousins we shall not surely know. John is known as the disciple whom Jesus loved; James acquired no distinction, not even a nickname, and died early in the days of the Christian movement at the hand of Herod Agrippa. Even so there are reasons for feeling that the affection in which the turbulent Simon Peter was held was, in some respects, warmer than that which bound his own cousins to Jesus.

It was not until the beginning of the second year of his ministry that Jesus effected a semblance of organization in the movement that was gathering about him. There had been a few who had been with him with little interruption since he embarked upon his ever-widening ministry of healing and teaching. And within this small circle there were these three men who, it seems, had come to share his heart and mind as intimates. When Jesus saw the necessity of consolidating his strength by ordaining twelve of his followers, it is likely that the counsel of these three was sought and the names decided upon in the night-long conference on the hill above Capernaum. If this occasion provided them the vision of the transfigured Master—and there is evidence to support the idea—it may supply us with the reason for the failure to include the full fellowship in that important revelation.

This privilege and responsibility of intimacy with Jesus was never more vivid in their experience than on the Mount of Transfiguration and in the Garden of Gethsemane. Only of men who had thus entered the arcanum, could the uttermost of fidelity have been expected and asked. And yet their failures, both on the mountain and in the garden, were spectacular.

To be sure the misunderstanding on the mountain was not critical in the acute sense. They were so awed by what they saw that the only word spoken was a floundering sort of proposal that they take up at least temporary residence in the vicinity where this cavalcade of the immortals was passing. This, of course, missed the whole point, and Jesus was quick to hurry them down to the levels where life demanded not wonder among the shades, but work among the sick. It was only after some months that the explanation of the glorious vision made itself clear to them.

The affair in the garden, however, was different. There they were not witnesses of the glory of their friend in a blinding and transfiguring light. They were silent and stunned observers—if they saw anything at all—of the desperation of their friend in the half-light of shadows cast by the thick foliage of olive trees under the pascal moon. Here their defection was fateful, and inspired in their disappointed friend the famous words, "spirit willing, flesh weak." This was a mild rebuke, far gentler than their faithless somnolence deserved.

What of these three, particularly James and John? It is not difficult to paint their portraits. They were, we assume, successful men before they abandoned their boats and their hired help to follow Jesus. That is something in their favor. And their success was doubtless due as much to an aggressiveness of character as to the capricious fortunes of their trade. Competition was keen on the lake, and the industrious man won out. Those who, on a body of water famous for its sudden and violent displays of wind and storm, could suggest by occasional acts the nickname "the thunder boys," were certainly not placid and indecisive men. If they had joined themselves to their carpenter cousin because of blood ties only, they would not likely have grown as intemperate as the record makes them out when the importance of their movement was occasionally challenged or insulted. There was, in the course of their travels, a Samaritan village in which they sought a night's lodging for the fellowship. Mayhap they felt that an earlier visit to another Samaritan village near the well of Joseph had laid some obligation on these sullen folk that they might willingly discharge. In any event, their refusal to receive them—and they were the messengers of the one who in the other village had been entertained for several days because of what he had done for them—stirred their resentment to the point of proposing that fire from heaven be employed to destroy them. This was a rash and angry proposal, to be sure, but it bears testimony to their intense if undisciplined loyalty to the movement they had so recently espoused.

Because some artists have portrayed John the beloved, leaning on the breast of his friend, as a languid or diffident person; and since, unhappily, we have come to think that Jesus would have found intimacy with a turbulent spirit disquieting to his own, we have softened the stern outlines of John's forthright character, and similarly, if we have thought about it, of James' also.

Is not a truer picture one that presents them as men who today would be called radicals? This is a disputed word among us, but has a right to its own dignity. Here were two men, successful and yet unhappy. As loyal sons of Israel, their material security had not satisfied their sense of spiritual hunger. To restore moral and spiritual vigor to their day, and to recapture something of the glory of their past was a dream they must have talked endlessly about as they plied the waters of the lake, or sat on the stony shore and mended their nets.

When their cousin from Nazareth fired their ready hearts with the vision of the Kingdom of God, and when they saw, through his eyes, the restoration of justice, love and equality in their own time, they felt no tie strong enough to restrain them from leaving all and following him. Less extreme than the fanatical Zealots, they nevertheless believed that there were occasions when fire from heaven was the sort of testimony their cause deserved. That Jesus loved John should not convert him, in our eyes, to a soft-voiced sentimentalist; rather should we say that because he was forthright and slow to compromise, Jesus loved him.

It is some such understanding of these men that makes their subsequent history intelligible. The death of James may have been the reward of an uncompromising spirit; and when Peter and John defied the city magistrate in Jerusalem in the days immediately following the reassembling of the scattered disciples, there was a defiance in their manner that puzzled the authorities as much as it angered them. Furthermore, it is such an understanding of these men that enables us to estimate the pathos of their failure in the garden, the surprise of their friend in their torpid and resistless sleep, and the grim austerity of the self-control in which he marched ahead, without them, to meet his destiny.

We are reminded again of the abnormal tension of those testing days, a tautness that even nature seemed to share and which broke finally in the storm that engulfed the hill of death the next day. To those who had withdrawn from the city after their frugal meal together, there may have been something in the breathless air of the night, in the strained and restless silences of their vigil that gave edge to their nerves; and stirred their minds with portents of evil. And we must therefore allow this tenseness to help us explain the unresponsiveness of these men to the critical anxiety of their beloved friend. It is not conceivable that they had changed their minds. It is rather that the anodyne of anxiety finally broke down their proud and incursive spirits, and left them powerless to aid him.

This surely is the reason that Jesus' rebuke was so gentle as to be almost a commiserating word. He had warned them that that very night the sheep would be scattered, and that there was treachery afoot. And when he mysteriously drew the three men aside and said directly to them: "My soul is crushed with anguish to the point of death," he was using language they had never heard from him before. His request of them was simple where it might, within reason, have been difficult. "Wait here, and watch," he said. Watch; it was the easy, and yet the all important thing. "Be vigilant," he meant, for such mischief as the shadows concealed might any moment break out. He had a struggle to make, one that was to engage all his faculties, and he wanted to depend on the eyes and ears of his friends to sound a warning when danger threatened.

And yet when three times he found them sodden in sleep, he spoke no word to reproach their almost criminal inadvertence. Many a sentry has been executed for sleeping on duty, but Jesus' word was one of pity, not of condemnation. This is what was meant when in an earlier chapter it was said that as he approached the cross his poise steadied. It would have caused no surprise if he had broken their slumber with a volley of bitterness and abuse. But there was only pain and disappointment, and even it was put in the form of a question as if to offer them a chance to explain. "Could you not watch with me one brief hour?" And then, as if to give them an excuse their sleepy wits could not have offered, he added: "The spirit is indeed willing, but the flesh is weak." At least, in this moment of their faithlessness, he credited them with good intentions to the last. Had it not been that he was aware of the strain under which they had already slumped, he would, in all likelihood, have spoken as he once did to Simon when he boasted of his bravery. The damage was done; it was too late. He had won a victory over his own spirit; the strain of anxiety and fear had won a victory over theirs; and as he finally shook them awake, the betrayer pushed his way toward him, through the darkness, and kissed him. In default of the alert devotion of true friends, the lips of treachery simulated love, and gave him over to his enemies.

It is characteristic of the ease with which we excuse ourselves, that the phrase: "The spirit is willing, but the flesh is weak" has become the phrase by which this incident is best remembered. "Not thy will but mine be done" is the language of devotion; but by the ratio of devotion to life, that phrase is less used than the other. Not only so. It is used by those who, otherwise fairly mature and well-behaved, seek to excuse every possible lapse from standards of probity. It is an ancient trick— to explain one's righteousness in terms of a rigid and rewarding discipline of one's own spirit; but to excuse one's evil as the weakness of the flesh. This poses an interesting moral question in itself. We may be allowed to wonder whether in later years as they reflected on it these men were as easy on themselves as Jesus was. It is doubtful. Had they accepted the easy way to excuse their failure in a critical hour, it is unlikely that they would have accepted the hard way to win their amazing spiritual victories in the next six months.

But our interest in this story must not linger any longer in the garden. It is poor solace now either to praise or blame these men. Rather would we remember them again for a moment as the Sons of Thunder instead of the sons of sleep, and be admonished ourselves, lest we too fail at another critical and strained hour to keep vigilant, and in our weariness or despair add our failures to the betrayals of these bitter days.

For the parallel between these radicals and the tired radicals of our times had already suggested itself. Perhaps in our present world context the word radical is too charged with emotion to be used happily. Here is one of the curious accidents that has befallen our tongue. A word has been taken that meant originally to go to the root of the matter, and been made to mean to go beyond even the last valid inference of the matter! So, a radical man is thought of less as one who digs, than as one who explodes. He is more interested in extravagant ends than in elemental beginnings. The observation concerning Jesus that every radical man has at one time or another made to the effect that he was the most radical person who ever lived, has done nothing to abate the suspicion that modern radicals inspire.

But in such a study as this it ought to be possible to use the word within the limits of moderation or even of piety. If James and John were radicals in the rudimentary sense of the word, it is not to the discredit of those who emulate them if they win the same designation. And after all, we are concerned more, for the moment, with tired radicals, and they, in nearly every situation, are quite harmless.

Is it not an amazing contrast that shows the same two men in the following situations? In the Samaritan village they propose to destroy a group of people who decline to put up their friend for the night. In the Garden of Gethsemane they allow themselves to go to sleep when they have been warned that treachery is stalking their friend. And yet it may be regarded as a fairly accurate picture of something that happens to many, if not to most of us.

Take for example the contrast between the radical experience of conversion—and whether it be gradual or cataclysmic it involves a radical spiritual change—and the sumptuous sleep of Christian living—or, if the phrase suits better, church membership. It casts no reflection on this essential change of life—motivation to say that in more cases than not, if we believe church statisticians, the ardent young heart that expressed its new-found joy by singing, "I'll go where you want me to go," ends up finally whispering, "I think I'll take a nap." That there are many to whom the Christian experience never ceases to be rooted in the roots of life, radical in the truest sense, is due the fact of the survival of the church. Radicalism has kept the church alive; though the contest between the radicals and the somnambulists, is always a spirited one. One forbears to comment here on what happens to the minister whose radicalism never fails him; and yet one cannot forbear to predict what will happen to the Christian movement when its radical leadership goes to sleep.

So common a circumstance is this decline of radicalism in the field of social and political action that it has created the phrase "tired radical" to classify those whose warm blood has succumbed to the anaesthetic of fatigue. The morning when these words were being written a syndicated newspaper column opened with a lament concerning the silencing of a one-time liberal voice in national affairs thus: ". . . was once a fighting liberal himself and helped to wrest his state from the control of the . . . two generations ago. I have thought of him as a hard fighter, as a practical politician, and as a warm-hearted and generous man. Up to now I have always felt that when the roll was called on any fundamental issue . . . would always be on the side of the angels." The able member of Congress; it seems, had gone to sleep in his garden. "Eternal vigilance is the price of liberty" is perhaps our most quoted political cliché. It may be well to quote the context from which the sentence, slightly altered, has been lifted. It was John Philpot Curran who said: "It is the common fate of the indolent to see their rights become a prey to the active. The condition upon which God hath given liberty to man is eternal vigilance; which condition if he break, servitude is at once the consequence of his crime and the punishment of his guilt."

It comes down to this: most of the mischief that plagues the world is due less to hypothetical original sin, than to the unholy alliance between malevolence and indifference. The vicious people in the world are numerically insignificant; the indifferent are like the sands of the sea for number. By the tireless enterprise of a few evil men, the apathy of the indolent has been turned to the personal and group advantage of the few. Sleep has become the unwitting accomplice of treachery. The forces of good in the world are immobilized less by their adversaries, than by their sleep. We have heard it endlessly said that if the church would wake up it might change the character of civilization in a decade. "Opiate of the people," is the cruel indictment Lenin laid against religion. It has a sharp point, for it cannot be honestly disputed that many religiously comfortable people choose Gethsemane for sleep, instead of the Samaritan village for fire.

And yet what can be done? It is not only historically authentic that the rebuke of Jesus to these sleeping friends was gentle past our understanding. It was also psychologically authentic. For what can one do with the tired radical except pity him? One's response to his weariness is disappointment, to his sleep, exasperation. Once the radical is quit of his enthusiasm he is quit; except in those occasional instances when he wakes suddenly as the bewildered advocate of reaction.

James and John retrieved their reputation, and passed out

of the record as the same radical and flaming spirits they were when they entered the story. This supports the judgment, so often proposed in these pages, that it was the enormous pressure of those history-changing days that determined their behavior. This does not mitigate the evil that their moment of somnolence invited. To imagine them as wakeful and alert during that fateful hour, as Jesus had admonished them to be, might make necessary a rewriting of traditional theology, or the creation of an entirely new theology in terms of what might have happened had they anticipated and checkmated Judas' move. This all lies in the area of conjecture and has little vital interest; but it may serve to suggest that history might have taken another course, if the tired radicals had not slept. When the pressure was off, and the inspiration of a new and unexpected manifestation of the presence of their friend gripped them again, they became the center of a new radicalism, the shock of which the world still feels when it allows its heart to become sensitive to spiritual truth.

There is interest in the fact that for James and John there was no subsequent rebuke as there was for Peter after his dramatic denial. At least the record contains no such episode. This may or may not be understood to reflect the judgment of Jesus on their failures. To us the denial of Jesus was no isolated and individual act. In one way or another, all the twelve were united in the abandonment of their friend to his enemies. But it may be true that these two brothers, closer by ties of kindred and of understanding, woke later to a realization that was to them a sufficient rebuke. For Jesus had not waited till the defection in the garden to warn the disciples that, in the words of Curran: "the condition upon which God hath given liberty to man is eternal vigilance." There was one notable occasion, months before, when in the idyllic and serene surroundings of open fields and a sight of the sea, he had told them a story. A man once sowed good seed in his field, he said, and at the end of an active day, he and his helpers lay down and slept. During the night, "while men slept" an enemy came and sowed tares among the wheat. When, in due time, the first shoots of green showed above the ground, the sower's men came to him and said, "Master, was it not good seed you sowed in your land? Where then do the tares come from?" The reply is familiar to our ears: "Some enemy has done this."

The parallel is so striking as to be inescapable: sleeping men, a field at night, and an enemy skulking through the darkness; sleeping men, a garden at night, and an enemy skulking through the shadows. The spirit indeed is willing, but the flesh is weak. He that hath ears to hear, let him hear!

Chapter VI: JUDAS ISCARIOT

The face of Judas twisted wryly as Jesus, kneeling in front of his couch, sprinkled water on his feet and dried them ceremoniously with the towel. He was on the point of saying something about the need for preserving one's own dignity when others were bent on discrediting it. He who acts like a slave will be worth a slave's price and be treated as a slave. But he held his tongue. Peter, reclining near him, had broken out with a bit of characteristic bombast when Jesus knelt before him, and the quick retort he got, especially the remark about one of the twelve being unclean, made Judas think it were better to keep quiet. It was not a pleasant thing to hear—being called dirty; especially when one prided one's self on one's fastidious habits. Little the Galileans knew about keeping clean!

As the evening wore on, he grew more sullen and was not roused from his brooding silence until he heard Jesus admit that things were not going so well. "Tonight," he said, with an air of finality, "the shepherd will be smitten, and the sheep will be scattered." He had come to realize it at last, Judas thought. The rest of them knew their danger; but he had refused to see what he was leading them into. Judas shifted uneasily. He was hungry, but the meager fare on the table was unappetizing. Jesus, at the other end of the room, was talking to three of the men who seemed greatly agitated by what he was saying. Judas got up, stretched nervously and moved toward the center of conversation. Perhaps, he thought, Jesus was enlarging on his doleful remark about the fate that waited them all. As he stopped alongside his couch, Jesus dipped a fragment of dry loaf into the dish and handed it to him. Judas took it gingerly, as if it were dangerous to touch. "What you are about to do," Jesus said quietly, "get done quickly." Judas felt overpowered by a weight of fear that was insupportable in the close atmosphere of the little room. Pushing the door open he went outside. He tossed the morsel of bread down the stone stairway, and then followed its bouncing, incalculable descent with careful though hurried footsteps.

As he stepped out into the narrow alley, the crowding walls of the houses seemed to lean toward him as if to trap him. He was stifled by their closeness. He broke into a shuffling trot, and the noise of his sandaled feet echoed behind him like the whispering of a pursuer. Presently he stopped under the light of a taper, perched high on a wall where two alleys intersected. He was breathing heavily, and stood for a moment, wiping his forehead with the back of his hand.

"No wonder," he thought viciously, "the sheep are to be scattered. When the shepherd turns into the slave of the sheep, he is no man to follow." He resumed his way, slowing his pace when he came to a wider street, where the moon lighted the stone pavement, and where there were others moving about unhurriedly. He felt safer in the broad spaces among people he did not know; and with his mind turning over and over the prospect of danger, and his secret plan to escape it before it broke upon him, he came at length to the bazaar of Annas, by the south wall.

The booths were closed, and business was done for the day. He walked aimlessly along until he came to a stall where, through the open door, he could see three or four men gathered beneath a light. Stepping up to the door, he looked in inquisitively. He was unobserved and stood wondering what they were doing when a squad of Roman soldiers, clearing the streets for the night, drew near. Judas, fearing a brush with these ruffians, stepped quickly inside and let the curtain fall. As the soldiers clattered by, one of the men turned and saw

Judas standing inside the door. He covered a pile of coins with both his hands and turned angrily and said:

"Who are you, and what right admits you here?"

Judas bowed nervously, twisted his tunic between his hands, and said:

"Judas, of Kerioth beyond the Wilderness of Moan, a half day's journey from the Salt Sea, the sea of Death."

Malchus laughed with evident relief. "A Judean! I thought for a moment, when I heard the hob-nailed hoofs of those Roman pigs that you were one of them, stepping in to snatch a fistful of tribute. The high priest has paid them well. He might not believe us if we told him they had robbed us too."

Judas looked at the pile of money on the table. It represented Caiaphas' share in the day's business in the booths, and was being counted before going into the high priest's coffers. Two of the three men had already counted it, and Malchus was waiting to check their totals.

"The day's business is profitable," Judas remarked ingratiatingly.

"Fair," said Malchus, "and if the Galilean comes no more to threaten the worshipers, Caiaphas will not lack for wine. But another riot like that three days ago and the old man will have to drink water." Malchus laughed at the prospect.

"You need not fear him," said Judas with a show of boldness. "He will come no more."

"No? It would be worth much to know you speak the truth."

"It is the truth; I swear it by the beard of Abraham."

"How do you know?"

"I am just come from his company. He and his friends are afraid to come to the temple again."

"Afraid? I should like to have proof of that," countered Malchus.

"They are truly afraid. They boast their courage, but they have no heart. And this very night I heard him say the shepherd would be smitten and the sheep scattered."

Malchus got up and faced Judas. He scrutinized him sharply in the yellow light that shone weakly from a lantern hung in the roof.

"How do I know you are not lying? Is it not said the Salt Sea dries up the honor in the heart of a Judean?"

Judas held up a wallet for Malchus to see.

"This is the Galilean's money. I hold the bag." He squeezed it convulsively and hid it again in his girdle.

"So!" drawled Malchus. "You are of his fellowship?"

"Nay," corrected Judas, "I was; but no more. If we are to be scattered, I shall choose my course for flight; and I shall at least have bread and figs till I am home again."

"How fares your business?" Malchus asked.

"Very ill. We had a chance five days ago when the multitudes acclaimed him. They put their garments on a beast and spread their robes in the dust for him. Had he the wits to see, he could have taken their last farthing. But he ——"

"Wait," interrupted Malchus. "If you speak the truth, you can perhaps be persuaded to tell us where he is."

"Aye—for a price."

"Nay, no money will we give you; why should we trust you? But mayhap you will take us to his hiding place."

"For a price," repeated Judas, "and more ——"

"What, pray, can you want more than a bribe?"

"You must furnish me aid. I dare not go alone. He is surrounded by eleven men. Some of them are rough, unimaginative louts from Galilee. One of them has a sword; there may be others with blades hidden in their girdles. And he, the Galilean, no one knows his strength. He boasts he has angel legions at his call ——"

Judas did not finish his sentence. Malchus had suddenly stepped outside and was gone. In the silence that followed his disappearance, Judas felt again the crushing, imponderable weight of fear returning to press upon his mind. What was this madness he had done? He had thought to flee the city and the coming terror, and here he stood in the company of those who sought to strike the Galilean down. Instead of escaping, he had trapped himself. He moved to the door. Looking back over his shoulder he saw the men, busy once again with their counting. Outside he heard footsteps, but before he could step through the door, Malchus appeared again. On his heels was a crowd of ruffians jostling each other for room for the free movement of the odd variety of swords and staves they carried. They were an ill-assorted and vulgar rabble, thieves, scavengers, camp followers, temple menials and street brawlers who liked nothing so much as a fight. They knew Malchus well, for as the agent of Caiaphas, he paid them both to riot or to keep the rabble in hand, as the need required. Malchus led them crowding into the small stall, and ordered one of the money counters to fetch a jar of wine from under the table.

As they quarreled over their drink, Judas was warned by an inner monitor to have nothing to do with them. He was about to move to the door when Malchus pulled his sleeve and said, expansively:

"Here are your men—your help; I had no trouble getting them. Name me your price; and I think that will be no harder to find than these were."

His noisy words evoked robust laughter and shouts of approval. But Judas was slow to speak. His mouth was strangely dry. He thought a sip of wine would help, but dared not ask for it. He clutched involuntarily at the wallet in his girdle, and sidled a step toward the door.

"Stop, you salt sea crab; we are not yet ready to go. Name me your price. Our gentle friends will have a score to settle with me, and you, if we forget our promises to them."

Judas looked at Malchus and at the ruffians. They were amused by Malchus' playful words, and perplexed at his warning. But when they turned their bleared and vinous eyes on Judas, he cringed and whined:

"I am not sure whither the Galileans will go to spend this

night. It is not yet the third watch. Better perhaps to wait, and on the morrow seek them in the temple."

"Your price," snarled Malchus; "or shall we pay you what we will?"

"The price? Yes, yes," stuttered Judas, "the price. Give me the price of a slave; one who washes the feet of those who come to feast—thirty pieces of silver."

Malchus picked up thirty pieces off the table and dropped them into Judas' wallet. He noticed that the hands of the betrayer trembled as the coins clinked into his dirty leather purse.

"The old man will be pleased at this," Malchus said, as he drew aside the curtain and ordered the men to start. Judas found himself immediately pushed forward until he was at the head of the mob. He looked at the moon, and licked his lips nervously. There had already been time enough, he thought, for them to have reached the Garden of Olives.

The wallet felt uncomfortably heavy against his side. He thought of a millstone, and of the depths of the sea, and shuddered.

THE MAN OF KERIOTH

The business of arriving at a geographical point is only slightly affected by one's point of departure. I can reach London from New York, Capetown, Calcutta or Shanghai. But the business of arriving at a spiritual point (allowing, for the moment, the contradiction) is significantly affected by the point of departure. If I set out for Understanding, and begin at Prejudice, Distrust, Hate or Ignorance, I shall most likely never arrive. I shall stoutly affirm, of course, that I have; but to one observing my peregrinations, it will be obvious that I have simply been moving in futile circles about the point where I began.

This latter fact is pertinent to a study of Judas Iscariot. His diabolical treachery has won for him the almost unanimous execration of history. No mother would dare to call her son Judas, though its more common form, Judah, meant "praise" and was once a noble name. We start at Judas from the standpoint of revulsion, contempt, or hatred, and when we reach him, he is in the nethermost pit of hell. And, lest we relent, we have allowed the place of his endless expiation to remain in the background of our minds as it was pictured by Dante.[1] Brutus and Cassius share his fate in the bloody jaws of the monster. Shakespeare has helped us to pity Brutus; and a breed of venal politicians has helped us understand Cassius. Judas alone evokes from us no extenuating sympathy.

And yet there have been efforts to arrive at an understanding of Judas by beginning at other points of view. Sympathy, sorrow, pity, and love have guided some attempts to reach him understandingly. These efforts, and the explanations they have produced, have not expunged his sin. They have, rather, accounted for his fateful act by circumstances as much external to himself as they are to us. It is not necessary to recount the

[1] After describing Dis, "the emperor of the woeful realm"—the ninth circle of Hell, Dante says:

> "The six eyes wept; and o'er his triple chin
> The tears and bloody foam poured fast around.
> At every month his teeth a sinner tore,
> E'en like a mill; so that within his jaws,
> Were three of them at once tormented sore.
> To him in front this crushing was but play
> Compared with what he suffered from the claws,
> Which from his neck oft tore the skin away.
> 'That one above,' to me the master said,
> 'Is Traitor Judas,' doomed to greater pangs:
> His feet are quivering, while sinks down his head
> Of the other two, whose heads are plunged below
> Brutus the one, who from the black throat hangs;
> See how he writhes, yet speaks not in his woe!
> Cassius the other, with such strength endued.'"

The Divine Comedy, by Dante. Translated by I. C. Wright (London: Geo. Bell and Sons).

vagaries of these efforts; this is only to note a humane spirit that extends even to history's most celebrated villain.

There is, in fact, more than a merely humane interest back of such studies. Since Dante and Milton gave to the common mind the pictures of a literal and local hell, the whole concept of the technic of retributive justice has greatly modified. The idea of a place of endless torment has given way to understandings of the nature of God and the necessity and nature of his judgment on sin, which, while no less severe and inescapable, provide a different framework for its operation. Therefore the abandonment of a literal and endless torment has left us with the necessity of finding new treatment for the man whose doom left him forever at the bottom of the pit. If a new idea has helped us extricate ourselves from the prospect of a Miltonic inferno, justice demands that we make it retroactive to Judas.

But more than this: we have come into deeper understandings about the nature of divine forgiveness. Why is Judas unshriven throughout eternity? Not because he was an impenitent betrayer; but because he betrayed the Lord of Glory. But if an immoral act is judged as such by principles and not by persons involved, why was a betrayal of Jesus any more heinous than a betrayal of Caiaphas might have been? An act of treachery against a current hero will arouse more popular anger than a similar act against a nameless beggar; but is it more wicked for that reason? Certainly not, unless moral judgments are contingent upon varieties in personality. Such a circumstance would make a mockery of all our standards of conduct. Indeed it has often done so; when, for example, it was no sin for a lord to kill a slave, or for a prince to seduce the daughter of a subject. It is true, therefore, to say that the moral quality of the act of Judas was not affected by the victim of it, however the passions of men may have been aroused by it. If Dante consigned him to the lowest circle of hell, he did so because of a sense of personal outrage, not because of a sense of abstract justice.

Hard cases make bad laws, say the jurists. And to prevent a recurrence of the crime of Judas, the law would affix a heavier penalty on the next culprit. But hard cases make the act of forgiveness noble. Here is, indeed, the essential difference between law and grace. "It is scarcely conceivable (from the standpoint of law) that anyone would die for a just man, although for a good man perhaps some one might have the courage even to die. But God gives proof of his love (grace) to us in Christ's dying for us while we were still sinners."[2] If justice demands hell for Judas; grace demands his redemption.

The theological tangle into which the betrayal of Jesus plunged the older theologians is too familiar to recount here; except to say that the effort to discover a necessity behind the deed which, in order to make a scheme of redemption possible, forced Judas into action, plays dangerously with morals. If his treachery was necessitous in the nature of things, then his act was amoral; since no act is moral that is involuntary. To say that Judas consented to complicity in an act some ultimate destiny demanded, blunts, but does not remove the horns of the dilemma. How could God punish one whose sinful act was integral to his redemptive scheme? Or, if it had no place in an original plan, was not the use of Judas' treachery pure opportunism? It was this problem that agitated the theological mind of former days and resulted in explanations that were sometimes as fantastic as they were devout. That this difficulty is a very old one may be suggested by the fact that Luke's account of the betrayal makes Judas out as the guide of the arresting party, omitting from the story his kiss and overt participation.

When we go back to the record itself, we find grounds for a study of the sin of Judas that lie deeper simply than the humane impulse, or the formal statement of doctrines of for-

[2] Romans V:7-8; Weymouth's translation.

giveness. In the mind of Jesus there is only one barrier to un-
limited (70 $\times$ 7) forgiveness; and that rests upon the unfor-
giving spirit of the one seeking pardon. "If ye do not forgive,
neither will your father which is in heaven forgive your tres-
passes."[3] Are there exceptions to this? If the answer is yes,
then some power, arbitrary to the point of violating moral
standards names them; if the answer is no, Judas is forgivable
if he complies with the requirements. And is the limit that
confines to the soldiers the prayer of Jesus for the forgiveness
of those who killed him, justifiable? Unless Judas is thought
to have been the only rational and deliberate participant
among all those who, in those last six days, conspired unwit-
tingly to yield their friend up to death, then in principle, as
well as in fact, Judas should be allowed to come within the
compass of that prayer.

Of course Jesus called Judas a devil, but he called Simon
Peter Satan. In fact, except in the place where Judas is called
a thief, he is everywhere said to have been possessed by a devil.
The interesting fact emerges, that demon possession in the
New Testament is almost always descriptive of illness.[4] It is
not used to denote wicked or perverse impulses. Paul, whose
sensitiveness to the causes and manifestations of sin and the
processes of redemption led him into deeper and wider ranges
of thought on the matter than any of the New Testament
writers, ignores Judas entirely except indirectly in a phrase:
"On the night in which he (Jesus) was betrayed." It may be no
more than rhetoric; but it is interesting, at least, that Paul
names himself as the chief of sinners, usurping the dubious
honor that we have given to Judas. When Luke wrote The
Acts, he described the betrayer's defection as a fulfillment of
scripture, as Matthew—with his fondness for proof-texts—does.
Was this not the result of reflecting on the significance of the
act, an effort to extenuate it, instead of an emotional revulsion

[3] Mark XI:26.
[4] The Gadarene demoniac was a crazy man, not a wicked one.

to it? It would seem to be the case that we who have judged Judas theologically, instead of morally or psychologically, have made a good deal of trouble for ourselves.

What happens when Judas is studied psychologically? Certainly not that his sin ceases to be reprehensible and desperately tragic. In spite of the fact that some psychologists distrust and disbar the word, sin still stubbornly refuses to be explained away. Never, in spite of psychology, has the brutal fact of human sin been more palpable and open than in our times. But we have come to understand some manifestations of this hateful thing as illness of the mind, and to treat it so. The witches who were once burned by the pastors are now given occupational-therapy by the psychiatrists.

We have made much throughout these studies of the fact of mental strain, and sought to cast the light of that fact over the events that have engaged us. None escaped its evil influence, not even Jesus who struggled with it until his victory in Gethsemane, and his emergence into the incredible calm of his last desperate hours. He warned them at the supper table: "This night all of you will turn against me";[5] and all of them did, in various degrees and ways of repudiation. What, we are entitled to ask, was the psychological background of Judas' act?

It was clearly different from that of his fellows. We need only to take the traditional account of his background to see this. The following sentences are lifted from such an estimate, one that represents the conservative theological viewpoint.

He was the only one of the twelve apostles outside of Galilee, and this fact may have played its part in the final breach between him and the rest. He was a man of business habits, for he became the treasurer of the group, and finally a thief. There is no doubt that Judas aspired to be the leader of the twelve apostles, next to Jesus, and some scholars think that he really was the head of this body of wonderful men. . . . The reasons

[5] Matthew XXVI:31.

that led Judas to betray Jesus were probably many. He looked for a political Messianic Kingdom, and was greatly depressed by Christ's talk about his death. His hopes were probably aroused by the glory of the triumphant entry of Christ, but they were rudely dispelled by the final breach with the authorities in the temple and by the doleful discourse on the Mount of Olives about the destruction of Jerusalem and the end of the world. And then Jesus set a date for his death, after two days; and at the feast of Simon, in Bethany, he allowed Mary of Bethany to waste a deal of money on ointment, and gave a sharp rebuke to Judas for his objection. This was the last straw on the camel's back. In a rage of resentment, disappointment and jealousy, Judas got up and went to the Sanhedrin and offered to betray Jesus to them during the feast for thirty pieces of silver, the price of a slave.[6]

There are certain intimations in this account that are important: the breach between Judas, a Judean, and the Galileans; his aspirations to leadership, and his sense of power as the treasurer; hopes of a Messianic Kingdom, depression caused by talk of death and the end of the world; estrangement of the temple authorities; the waste of money and the mortification of rebuke. These various states of mind resulted, we are told above, in a rage of resentment, disappointment and jealousy.

Obviously these provide a picture of tension; but the impetus that touched off the fateful act may have been none of these. Indeed, resentment, disappointment and jealousy are hardly sufficient to account for his behavior before, during, and after the betrayal. Add, therefore, to the concoction, the volatile ingredient of fear.

At once a question is raised. Peter was afraid, and so were those who took to their heels in the garden. But what evidence is there for fear in Judas' heart? Little, if it be the fear that reacts only as panic. Terror, the most spectacular type of fear, is also the least frequent. For every one who runs away in

---

[6] *The System Bible Study*, p. 25. Chicago, Illinois.

panic, there are thousands who stand their ground and absorb
the poison of fear into their mental tissues. The shocks that
buffet them are seismic tremors; they rarely break into cataclysmic violence. They are the victims, in modern psychological jargon, of anxiety neuroses. But it is fear, nevertheless.

Observe the pattern of this anxiety as it is presented in the
description quoted above. Judas must have had some measure
of faith in the wisdom and integrity of his friend. When,
therefore, Jesus talked about the destruction of Jerusalem, the
end of the world, his own death and the scattering of the fellowship, Judas would have been a phlegmatic or an inattentive
soul had he not felt the tingle of danger run along his nerves.
But deeper than that afferent sensation was a groundwork of
misgiving in Judas' mind. He had come north from Judea
where he was a man of some importance and means. Looking
toward a rejuvenation of the moribund hopes of his people,
he had put his living into the enterprise,[7] in the assurance that
he was giving himself generously toward the long-hoped-for
restoration of the national power of Israel. But he had gradually come to see his hopes diminish, the glory he had foreseen,
engulfed in the forecast of the destruction of the holy city.
And if he was a thoughtful man, he very likely found his spirit
oppressed by a sense of frustration. He had left all for the cause
of the Galilean. The folk in Kerioth-Hezron may have sought
to dissuade him, or even laughed at him when he left. Now
his money was gone; his dream of power—worthy or otherwise,
no matter here—was dimming in the dawn of a rude awaken-
ing. Suppose he went home; scorn would greet him. But while
he stayed, the destruction of the world impended!

It may not be mistaken to ascribe to Judas one of the mo-
tives that inspired the hearts of some of the prophets, of

[7] Cf. the word of Simon Peter in Mark X:28, "We have left all and followed Thee," and its context. It follows the refusal of the Rich Young
Ruler to sell all his goods and have treasure in heaven; and is followed
by the promise Jesus extended to those who had left father and mother,
houses and lands, etc., for the sake of the gospel.

earlier days. The margin that separates a noble from a base
act is often thin as a knife blade; and the loftiest idea balances precariously on it until it tips one way or the other.
Habakkuk once cried: "When I heard, my heart trembled;
my lips quivered at the voice: rottenness entered into my
bones, and I *trembled in myself that I might rest in the day
of trouble*."[8]

However this may be, it is apparent that the seismic tremors
—the anxious sense of fear and frustration—presaged an earthquake. All about him were men in various states of nervous
excitement. The Galilean had tried to comfort them, promis-
ing them a soon-to-be-prepared place of safety, and offering
them peace such as the world of turmoil could not grant. Perhaps he had talked with Jesus, disclosing to him his disappointment and his unstable mind. He may, in desperation,
have threatened his friend. There is clear indication that
Jesus knew what he was contemplating, though he did not
reveal it, lest it add to the disquiet of the group. The story
tells us, significantly, that the devil entered him. Was it the
demon of fear that had haunted some of the others and had
once driven two thousand swine down the slope into the sea?
He was on his feet in one instant, and through the door into
the night in another. The tremor in his harassed soul shook
him menacingly, toppling every dream and ideal about him
in chaotic disorder. The violence increased. He makes his offer
to the agent of the high priest. There is a din as of the rum-
blings of doom about his ears. For a moment it stops, breath-
lessly. There is a moment of incredible calm in a garden—and
a kiss. Then the storm again. To the sense of frustration is
now added the black cloud of guilt, and the fear of retribution.
He had betrayed innocent blood. Then the flight back to the
city, the silver coins thrown at the feet of the astonished priests,
the panting escape through the city gate, to a field, and to a
gallows tree. And driven to the last excess of fear, as his life

[8] Hab. III:16.

is choked out of him, the earthquake breaks in a tumult of frenzy. It was such a cataclysm as the world had never seen, for it marked the end of an era, and the days that followed brought with them a new destiny for the race.

If this did happen, we still have no reason for viewing the betrayal of Jesus as anything less than the tragedy it has always been. If it might have happened otherwise, we have no reason, except an inclination to explore the hypothetical, to continue our study. Certainly Judas will remain as the basest of traitors, though he no longer is to be found in the frozen pit of Cocytus, torn forever in the bloody jaws of Dis.

But surely it must serve to bring to mind something of the destruction that fear accomplishes in our own times. What elevated and ennobling monument to human enterprise is not cast down by its violent shakings? Cannot this age be truly characterized as the great age of fear? And is there any denial or betrayal that escapes this growing psychosis? Democracy is betrayed by those who fear it, or themselves; God is betrayed by those who have lost faith in him; culture is betrayed by those who fear that wisdom is weakness and that art is a symptom of decadence. And in these times Jesus Christ is betrayed, not by those who hate him, but by those who have had the warmth of an early experience chilled by a suspicion that he no longer is the way, the truth and the life. The parallel between our times and the days of our Lord's passion is striking in many ways, but in none more than this: alongside their apprehensive world, the death of Jesus and the scattering of the disciples, we set, in slightly different language, as we read the craven spirits of our days, the destruction of civilization, the death of moral idealism, and the panic and disorganization of the people in the face of the organized wickedness of the world.

One is tempted to press the parallel further, and observe that it was a betrayal that opened the gates through which new hosts of victorious spirits have marched down the ages. We may, if we have that perspective which is the essence of true Christian optimism, gain some comfort from such contemplation. It may happen again. But such thoughts are wide of the compass of our study. Let us rather return briefly to Judas, this strange man who shared the passion of Jesus.

Sinner he undoubtedly was, and so are we all, by much the same rule as that by which we must judge him. He could not love because he was afraid. "There is no fear in love, for perfect love casteth out fear." There is a simple formula which gives sharpness to the proposition: Fear equals betrayal; love equals courage.

Are we, after all, afraid? Not physically; for man today is capable in an emergency of prodigious feats of courage. Is it not that we are moral cowards? Or to put it in the language of the record, has perfect love cast out fear? Here is the heart of all betrayals, whether of the man of Kerioth or the man of Chicago. Henceforth in our moments of anxiety we shall remember a garden and a kiss. We shall not excuse Judas Iscariot, nor shall we lightly excuse ourselves.

Chapter VII: SIMON PETER

A Fisherman Afraid of the Sea

R ock," said Simon the Zealot, contemptuously; "to call Simon, son of Jonas, a rock is to insult rocks in general." He slapped the massive stone on which he was sitting. Around him in the semi-darkness the resting forms of seven men were dimly visible. Peter, James and John were out of earshot under a heavy shadow of olive trees. Jesus was a stone's throw beyond them. What had happened to Judas Iscariot no one seemed to know. It was the rest of the twelve who were grouped around the Zealot.

"Guard well your words, Simon," warned a voice hid by a shadow. "How do you know there is no enemy close enough to hear you?"

"Enemy?" Simon stood up and counted slowly, pointing to each recumbent figure. "We are seven here; there is no enemy except he be one of you," he answered sourly.

"Seven, indeed," the voice continued quietly, "but during the last watch of the night did not one leave us? And he is gone we know not whither, though I, for one, fear the worst."

"Fear?" retorted Simon, his voice rising, forgetful of the admonition to silence, "Fear! That's the trouble, always fear. And what is it tonight that rattles your feeble shanks? Is it the late hour, and this patch of shadow? Is there none that can stand up but me? Can you not keep your knees from smiting save by lying down?"

"Your friend the Rock is not afraid," came another voice. "Less than two hours ago did he not say that no matter if all of us should forsake the Master, he would stand by him?" The Zealot detected that a sneer inflected the words.

"Bah," he snorted in reply; "the Rock will not flee? Mark you; this night we may see a strange sight—a rock that runs." He laughed roughly at his crude jest.

"Is it well that you should talk of your own courage while you laugh at another's boast?" Andrew had risen slowly to his feet. He was standing about ten paces behind the rock by which the Zealot stood. There was no rancor in his voice, neither were his words angry or pained. Simon the Zealot turned his body halfway around and faced his questioner. Andrew continued:

"My brother speaks hasty and boastful words ——"

"Aye; but he speaks not only for himself. Before he boasts of his own courage, he must accuse us of cowardice."

"Truly spoken," answered Andrew. "I cannot defend him; but I can explain him." There was something in the steadied and subdued manner of his speech that quieted the group. "This is no place to boast of our bravery, nor is it the time to rebuke the rash promises of others. These are hours that shake the hearts of the stoutest men. It is no evil thing to be afraid. He who knows not fear, knows not courage. He only is brave, who, threatened by fear, yields not his heart to it."

There were low murmurs approving these quiet words. Andrew was little given to speech, and the men who were surprised by his mild rebuke to the Zealot, felt themselves also sobered by his moderation and his wisdom. He was so little like his erratic and outspoken brother that it was not infrequently whispered among his fellows that he deserved his brother's sobriquet. Simon was more like sand; it was Andrew who was massive, immobile, and silent as a rock. That his name meant "manly" was singularly fitting; nor was the fact forgotten that his brother's name meant "a hearing," by those who accused him occasionally of listening to things to which other ears were deaf.

The ill-temper of the Zealot had subsided as suddenly as it had arisen; and he sat down again on the stone. His manner of speech was hardly less volatile than the man he had been abusing. More than once he had been twitted that the reason he disliked Peter was that he was so like him. He saw in Peter disagreeable qualities that he would not confess in himself.

"How did it come about that you and Simon are so different?" It was Thomas who put the question.

"It is not strange," replied Andrew. "It must, I agree, seem odd to one who is a twin; but is it not true that blood brethren are, more often than not, as different as Cain and Abel?"

"Perhaps," Thomas answered. "Strange are the ways of God."

"Yes; but we do not always reason well to say that such differences are the doings of God's hands. To argue thus is to lay both blame and praise at the same altar."

"Yet who but God can order the making of a man?"

"That no one can surely say. But the fire and the vaunt you like not in my brother is surely not the handiwork of God. Did not the Master bid him be called Rock to undo the bungling error of another?"

"This is strange talk," broke in the Zealot, "such as I have not heard before. Do we judge him unkindly, not knowing him well?"

A faint sound of conversation drifted from the direction where Jesus and the three had withdrawn. It sounded like the voice of one in distress. The men stopped speaking, and for a brief interval, held their breath, listening. The murmur was repeated. It was clearly the sound of agonized speech, but the words were indistinguishable.

"Does he plead with an interloper?" one asked.

"Nay; I think he prays," came a whispered answer.

The sound died away. A gust of humid air rustled the olive leaves, and a drifting mantle of thick cloud veiled the face of the declining moon.

"Simon's bluster is a mask for fear." Andrew's voice retrieved the group's wandering attention, and brought them back from a confusion of pity and apprehension to renewed interest in their comrade. "When he was quite a small child, one day, trying to lean too far over the gunwale of a boat to see the men pull in a net, he fell into the sea. Fortunately for himself he dropped into the net, and that saved him. But it broke a great hole in the net and lost most of the fish. When he was finally pulled aboard, half full of water and quite full of fright, one of the men scolded him angrily and told him it was a demon of the sea that had pulled him in. For years after that he would not get into a boat. In fact, it was not until he was fully grown, and it was necessary that he make his living either fishing or at some other craft, that he could be induced to leave the shore."

"Did he ever get over his fear?"

"Well, the strange thing is that he never acknowledged being afraid of anything. The older he grew the more ways he discovered for avoiding dangerous situations; and whenever he got into the neighborhood of trouble, he would invariably talk noisily about his deeds of valor."

"But how could such a coward become a fisherman? It is not the safest of lives—not on the Sea of Galilee."

"Perhaps it was fear of starving to death," laughed the Zealot.

"Do you remember," Andrew broke in, "when we were caught alone in the storm on the sea? What a night it was! We hardly dared to hope that any of us would reach the shore alive. And then the Master appeared near by. You did not notice it perhaps, but I watched Peter during the height of the tempest. He whined and gibbered like a lunatic, but managed to keep mumbling an improvised incantation, as was his habit."

"And then the Master—" Thomas spoke up.

"Yes, the Master! Simon suddenly coming to his senses resolved that the stigma of fear should not attach to him, and asked to be allowed to walk on the water! He, who of all men feared the water most, wanted to step out on it! That, I think, was the most daring thing he ever did to disguise his fear."

The cloud that had mantled the moon for a darkening interval passed, and the pallid light, sifting through the trees showed the figures more distinctly. Andrew was smiling. On the faces of the others a sense of momentary respite from their anxiety, softened the lines etched by weariness.

"Then you think," asked the Zealot, "that his boast early in the evening was no honest offer of loyalty in the event of trouble?"

"Certainly not dishonest," answered Andrew, "but it is exactly what those of us who grew up with him would expect."

"And yet I do not understand," said Philip, "why the Master should call him Rock. He cannot know him as you do. You would surely give him no such name."

"I am not sure that he does not know him better than I do," answered Andrew. "Simon is bad enough now, but he is a different man from the fisherman who feared the sea. And it was the Master himself who taught me to understand and love a blood brother I had misunderstood and hated."

"Hated?" echoed the Zealot in surprise.

"Yes, hated," said Andrew humbly. "One day I heard the Master talking with him after one of his fiery outbursts. 'Satan has desired you,' he told him, 'that he might sift you as wheat. But I have prayed that your faith fail not.' I asked him afterward what he meant. 'Satan is the spirit of fear,' he said. Simon was once Satan to me; he was trying to frighten me. The Satan of fear is the father of a whole brood of sins, those sins of passion that are committed in hot blood ——"

Andrew did not complete his sentence. The other men were so intent on what they were hearing that Jesus and the three were almost in their midst before they saw him. His three companions were rubbing their eyes like bewildered children roused suddenly in the deep of the night. Jesus walked with a firm and vigorous step and stopped at the side of the stone where the Zealot had been sitting. All of the men rose instantly to their feet and followed the direction in which the hand of the Master pointed. The dancing light of a lantern leaped back and forth amid the trees, stopping every now and then like a discarnate spirit searching the darkness. As it leaped again, the noise of many voices hummed about it. The men looked at each other anxiously in the dimness.

"Let us be going," Jesus said, "the hand of him that betrays me is near." He began walking steadily toward the interlopers, as if to acknowledge the drunken courtseyings of the lantern. For ten paces he walked alone. The disciples stood drawn close together by the sense of sudden peril. Simon Peter stepped out of the circle and followed Jesus. His mind was like a vortex of spinning devils. He was choking with terror. In half a dozen stumbling strides he accosted the man carrying the lantern. Malchus was his name, the servant of the high priest. The fear that palsied Peter's mind gave the strength of desperation to his arm. Blindly he struck out. In his fist was gripped the hilt of a broad sword. The man with the lantern staggered as a heavy blow split his ear. As he fell forward, the light went out, and the wild confusion was muffled by the darkness. The only sound was of heavy feet running through the olive trees.

FEAR

The fascination of the three denials of Simon Peter is all but irresistible. Like the weaving hands of a mesmerist they so charm our eyes that our gaze is averted with difficulty. And even though we look away in revulsion or in shame, we will surely return again, drawn by the wonder and the pity of it all.

If the episode is studied from the standpoint of its dramatic fitness in the story of the last week, it is obviously an awkward bulge in the smooth movement of the narrative. We who are familiar with the record are unconscious of this disproportionate allocation of space to an irrelevant matter—irrelevant, if considered solely from the dramatic viewpoint. Peter as one of the dramatis personae is enlarged out of all proper perspective. He deserves no such prominence, a prominence that appears almost to have been maliciously granted in order to blacken his character. But, above all other considerations, is the fact that the issue of the story is unaffected by his perfidy. The betrayal was the evil deed of another, and the sentence of death was to be pronounced by Pilate. It is unlikely that anything hapless Peter could have done would have changed the issue already determined by other forces. Indeed had the whole episode been left out of the story, there would have been no appearance of omission or oversight in the dramatic sequence.

Furthermore the story sounds unreal. Here was a man whose intimate friendship with another had been unspoiled by suspicion or disloyalty. To be sure there had been misunderstandings, and even the exchange of bitter words. But Peter was neither soured by rebuke nor dispirited by bewilderment. His attachment was a brusque and sometimes fumbling sort, but no hint of deceit or disaffection sullied it. How then can one account for the out-of-character behavior of this important actor as the play draws to its denouement? It was not introduced to restore flagging interest in the story; nor was it a final revelation of a villain's true character so long dissembled by disguise and trickery. It simply is not the artistic thing to do; it introduces an irrelevant anticlimax. We would feel, if we encountered a similar dramatic *tour de force* elsewhere than in the sacred record, that it was not true to life. People do not do that sort of thing. The dramatist either was inaccurate in his earlier portrayal of Peter's character, or he destroyed him, near the end of the story, out of spite.

All this is to be said if our study of the episode is to be made from a narrowly artistic angle. The wisdom of art would lay its veto against the propriety of its inclusion in the drama. But, strange to say, the heart of the world has not so studied it. From a wisdom, deeper and more vital than the wisdom of art, has been drawn an understanding that has carried with it the moral compulsions to which art remains indifferent. Somehow we meet this unhappy man on ground familiar to us all. We hear his stupid and profane denials and are shocked; we see him stumble out of the courtyard, shaken by an agony of contrition, and we weep with him. Here to the sensitive spirit is the epitome of all infidelities, the compendium of all denials.

It is not the weakness of humanity that we see here displayed, for Simon Peter was not a weak man. He had moments when vagary and vacillation unsettled him; but the solid ground of his character was rocklike. A weak man could not have won the immortality for which his name is guarantee.

If it is not weakness, what then is our clue to understanding? We return to the fact of tension which is adduced to explain much that is discussed here. Those days of our Lord's passion, days that changed the course of history, were electric with fear—fear that appeared in manifestations ranging all the way from misgiving to wild panic. And the tension caused by fear is physically as well as psychologically toxic; and when it is sustained, immobilizes the rational processes to the point, often, of insanity. Simon Peter, like his less famous companions, was afraid. Except we keep that in mind, we shall have no adequate understanding of his spectacular failures. With this fact before us, we attempt a reconstruction of the story.

There is nothing but imagination to help us account for Peter's attempt to arm himself with a sword. Unskilled in the use of such a weapon, he must have been a mildly amusing sight as he picked it up, in a shop or a friend's home, and tried its heft with a practice gesture. But it was certainly fear that induced him to possess it; and fear that led him to conceal it in the folds of his tunic. The surprise of Jesus at his rash violence in the garden must have been great. That he was aware such immoderation was dangerous to them all is evident from his warning after ordering Peter to put up his sword. "They that take the sword shall perish by the sword" had immediate as well as eternal relevance. It is to be expected that the cumulative fear that began, perhaps in Peter's nature, and was certainly aggravated in his experiences during the previous five days, and which was to run the gamut from anxiety to terror, was not to be purged by that soft-spoken remonstrance of his friend. Nor do the incidents that followed fail to confirm the fact.

John, known to the people in the courtyard of the palace of Annas, had returned to the company that was carrying Jesus thither. For a terrible moment, he and Peter had fled into the protecting darkness, but desperation or blind devotion had retarded their flight and returned them, and John entered the gate with the crowd. Peter lingered alone, and made his way timidly to the portal. He was beset by two fears: he was now separated from his scattered companions, and also from his friend. To return to the garden alone was hardly less formidable than to seek entrance into the court. At length he made his way to the door and rapped nervously. It seems that John, solicitous for his friend, had told the portress that another man would shortly be along, and having given her sufficient description to enable her to make an easy identification, asked her to admit him when he knocked.

When Peter's rap announced him, the woman drew the bolt and opened the gate sufficiently to give her a glimpse of the man. She surveyed him cursorily, and, in order to add his own word to her identification, asked him if he was not one of those who had been with the Galilean. She had no purpose but a kindly one. Her astonishment must have been considerable when he shouted a denial, but pushed his way past her into the safety of the enclosure.

He perhaps stood for an interval inside the gate. The woman left him to his own tortured reflections and went about her business. After all it was no affair of hers. And when the panic in Peter's mind subsided, seeing that he was, for a moment, out of the reach of danger, he moved quietly through the shadows to a place where a crowd of rough men were crowded about a charcoal fire, edging for advantage near its parsimonious warmth. To be among strangers was a better defense against fear than to stand alone in the darkness, so he joined them. For some time he was unnoticed. It was not until a serving woman, replenishing the fire, amplified the light till it fell on Peter's brooding face. By a chance, one of the men, seeing the stranger in their midst, asked him—with an impulse that was doubtless friendly—if he was not one of those in the recent fracas in the garden. At once the fear of detection that had been laid by the friendly encirclement of a high wall, leaped like a flame in the tinder of Peter's mind. And again he rudely rebuffed the rough cordiality of the man, and volubly denied any knowledge of what he had spoken of.

One can imagine the deflated spirit in Peter that observed no further pursuit of the question of his identity, and no follow-up of mischief. He must have felt rather much of a fool for his needless vehemence, if he was still impenitent for his improvident lie. But he was not to be let alone for long. His fear still shrouded him like an aura, and he was soon to be stifled by it again.

The crowd of men turned to their jesting, and Peter escaped momentarily from himself as he listened to their ribald chatter and noisy laughter. The dawn was stirring and the chill of the air was lifting as the light of the east began to break. The men drew away from the brazier; its glow was dimmed in the coming light and its warmth was all but spent. Still Peter stood near it, lost in the gloom and the growing chill of his own soul. He was roused suddenly by the servant who, returning with more fuel, spoke to him. She may have made some inconsequential remark about the need for a fire being past. At any rate she won from Peter a reply that betrayed, by his crisp accent, his Galilean origin. It was no evil intention that prompted the woman to ask him if he were not a Galilean, since his speech was clearly so. Indeed it may have been a gesture of kindness to a stranger that made her say: "So you are with that Galilean. Your speech gives you away." She smiled as she spoke, but not so Peter. Once again the tongue of fear leaped like a searing flame, blinding him with hot defensive resentment. And at the amazed woman he shouted with an oath: "No, I don't even know what you are talking about." At that moment there was a movement on a near-by balcony. The light of the new day was dim, but Peter saw a face that blinded his eyes like the sun at noontide. Atop the wall a cock stretched his neck and crowed to greet the day. The sound of that raucous note smote Peter's ear like the crack of doom, and he fled in terror from the courtyard.

It was a wretched performance, one which would have been the ruin of a weaker man than Peter. That he rose to sainthood afterwards is testimony to the authentic character of his nickname. But saintliness was no achievement of an hour. He did not rebound from his precipitate drop and come to rest on the pedestal where history has finally placed him. His recovery is a story all of its own and, could all the links in its chain be found or forged, would be one for the case book of the psychiatrists.

When we turn from the story to an effort to explain it we discover at once that the cause of Peter's denials was external to the circumstances that evoked them. Nothing in the encounter at the outer portal was provocative of his ill manners or his implausible lies. Nothing in a group of tough-minded and horny-handed men about a fire was terrifying to one inured to the harsher moods of nature, and accustomed to daily contact with fishermen and peasant folk. And what in the pleasantries of a servant wench busy about impersonal duties should have invited violence and profanity? It was, rather, something Peter carried in his turbulent soul. He felt its surge at the gate, by the fire, and in the presence of the servant. It was fear, deep and implacable. And it was not until that poison was purged, that dark sea drained, that restless demon exorcised, that he could achieve the poise and the victory of his later years.

Since there were three outbursts of this insurgent temper, there would seem to be three distinct ways in which his fear rose to assault and batter down the citadel of his loyalty to his friend.

The first was a fear that the thing to which he had given his devotion was powerless to sustain the full weight of life. After the sharp encounter in the garden, and the momentary escape into the night, it is possible that, left alone for a short while, there swept over him a doubt as sinister and engulfing as the darkness. That doubt had been expressed by others during the past few hours, and the experience of the past few minutes had brought no reassurance. Jesus had won a large following by kindness, but when he talked about "love to the uttermost" and "cross-bearing," the multitudes had melted like the snows of early spring. But Peter and the others had held on. The ideal of the Kingdom of God, the efficacy of moral love, the healing balm of forgiveness, what had happened to them? Suppose they were after all only the fancy of a dreamer. Were not the boats that had been left idle by the seaside these many months a safer craft in troubled waters than the promises and hopes of a carpenter? Suppose this teacher had misunderstood the nature of man, his greed, his grossness and his stupidity; and instead of winning men to beauty was to succumb to their cruelty and hate. Suppose! And with the mounting aggregate of doubt rose the potency of fear. He moved nearer to the gate; behind him was the darkness of doubt and terror, before him was— When the gate opened to his desperate knock and the woman's voice suggested definitely, though without intent, his faith in an ideal incarnate in a person—a person now lost to him, and an ideal now slipping away—little wonder that he cried out his denial. Who can with humility say he would have done any less?

The second way in which his fear assaulted his loyalty is an extension of the first. If he had questioned the value of an ideal and feared for himself because of his espousal of it, was it not natural, in the company of gross men, to doubt and fear its availability for their kind? He stood aloof for a moment beyond the circle about the fire. These men were salty of speech and boasted of their ruggedness. They dearly loved a brawl, and when not fighting, were noisily recalling their escapades, to impress each other. What was a lily of the field to them? Suppose it was more splendid than Solomon. Who cared about Solomon except as the paragon of lusty manhood? Forgiveness seventy times seven? A fist were better and more economical of time and patience.

There are, Peter might have argued nervously to himself, some to whom lilies and birds and forgiveness and that sort of thing were appealing. Take Nicodemus, for example. He no doubt understood talk about spiritual births and such like. He had time to think about them since he had no worries about food and clothing. He could seek the Kingdom of God without any risk; he had all the other things already. But these insensitive ruffians? If they wanted to pick up such ideals, would not the hard hands of necessity wrest them from their grasp? The aggregate of doubt was rising, and the chill of fear was numbing his soul. He moved nearer to the circle. The light broke over his face; the question was put to him. It is absurd that he ever should have been taken in by such delicate and impractical nonsense. "No," he shouted, "I don't know what you are talking about."

So may we move on to the third denial. He doubts and fears the ideal as an absolute value; he doubts and fears its practical usefulness among the mass of common men. But there still is a sector where the battle rages. What is he to do now? He has made a conspicuous failure. His more realistic friends were at least out of danger. They might be on their way to their homes. They had talked about such a move. But here Peter was, left by his friends and having denied his allegiance to their leader. He was neither out nor in. Unable to overtake his companions, he was equally unwilling to confront his friend.

What to do? Obviously look out for Number One since his friends were gone and the Master was in the hands of enemies. Take care of himself. The men revolted him by their rude manners. After months of association with the Galilean he had no relish for the obscenities that interlarded their noisy talk. There was the fire. Its warmth, though meager, was ungrudging. The thing to do was to make himself comfortable for the moment, let things drift and see what happened. Peter was warming himself at the fire. It was an abandonment of himself to opportunism. The blood that had rushed in hot resentment in the garden, because of his friend's peril, was cooled now. He had better warm his own hands. Was he afraid, if he reflected on it, that his devotion to all that Jesus had stood for would ultimately leave him by a brazier of cold embers, lacking even the spark to kindle it again? Once more there was a word, a kindly word. But the time was passed for kindness. One must repudiate unequivocally all the nonsense about losing one's life in order to save it. Put another ember on the fire, fool! No, wench; I don't know what you mean. Never even heard of the man.

When it comes down to the matter of our own loyalty to the Galilean in this day, where else than in these three areas do we feel the assault of fear? When we think of this, our words concerning Simon Peter become less censorious. What about loyalty in general? Toward democracy, for example. Do we believe in it as an absolute ideal; do we think it will work with the masses of the world? Are we sure that if made universally operative, we would find our hands warmed, along with all other hands, at its fires? Little wonder that democracy is a by-word and a hissing among many whose hands have been blue with cold because the fires have been expropriated by those who have wealth and power. The world today echoes with denials of democracy. Why? The answer is that fear haunts the heart of the world; fear that no organized political program can and will bring security and peace to the hearts of mankind.

One might press the pertinence of such an inquiry into the fields of church loyalty, an area where denials are less vocal, but alarmingly general. Or into the field of personal morals, or of economic systems. There is almost no area where a fear—it has not yet reached panic intensity and with us may never get that far—does not inspire the repudiation of ideals by which we have lived and prospered. There is little point in growing hysterical about it. Where such reaction occurs it is only another symptom of the tension of our lives. The restoration of Peter began when he came within the radiant focus of a face; it continued when he broke his heart in penitence; and it was completed by a life of danger-defying service to the friend he had once denied.

But before this last step was possible there was an amazing bit of psychotherapy that was performed on him. It is so astonishing a circumstance that it needs at least brief mention.

Much has been written and more said about the final conversation reported as having taken place between Jesus and Peter by the side of the Sea of Galilee, in the early hour of dawning. The story is so familiar as to need no repetition here. What is the point of it? In the light of the emphasis that these pages have put on the fact of nervous tension and in this chapter on fear, it is easy to see that Jesus was touching with a healing finger, the sickness of his faltering friend. In order that fear should be purged, another emotion had to take its place. Fear cannot simply be exorcized; it has to be displaced by an emotion of equal power.

Now the opposite of fear is confidence, and confidence is the flower of love. To put it another way: love which is the antithesis of hate is the antidote for fear. This is so obvious as to be almost trite. We do not fear those we love; we can only love those we do not fear. "Simon, son of Jonas, lovest thou me?" This question thrice repeated should be heard as over against another question: "Simon, son of Jonas, what fearest thou?" In a man whose life was dominated by fear, Jesus proposed to substitute love for fear; and his gentle repetition was no doubt to induce a practice that Peter may well have indulged to the end of his days. When doubt and fear strove in later days for dominance, who knows but that he said again to himself the formula given him by the seaside: "Simon, son of Jonas, lovest thou me?" And with the answer: "Yea, Lord, thou knowest that I love thee," came the victory for love. And was it not John the Elder, one of the few close friends of Simon Peter in his early years, who wrote many decades afterwards: "There is no fear in love; for perfect love casteth out fear."

It is, in all simplicity and honesty of speaking, no great distance from the courtyard of Annas to the world of our day. Judgment is, as always, being passed upon Jesus of Nazareth, and in the courtyards of the world fear is doing its deadly work. Is this the reason for the rising doubts, and the furious denials that plague the air? And after that is answered there remains another question: Can our fears be cast out, save by perfect love?

Chapter VIII: PONTIUS PILATE

TROUBLED BY DREAMS

Procula, beloved wife of Pilate, woke with a start. For a full minute she stared at the canopy over her bed, until its outlines, gradually taking shape in the darkness, reassured her that she had been dreaming. Her sense of great relief manifested itself by a deep intake of breath, and a sharp, convulsive exhalation. She heard no sound in her room except the regular breathing of the slave girl sleeping on a low cot at the foot of the great bed. She lay still for a while, listening to the nocturnal scurry of tiny sounds that pattered like frightened feet over the vast carpet of silence. Presently the voice of the palace watchman drifted in from a distant parapet. It was the third watch, three hours yet till cockcrow.

She turned over and tried to fetch her departed sleep by tricks she had hitherto found successful. She marked the steady rhythm of her heart and counted a legion of soldiers parading through her mind in the slow tempo of her pulse beat. But the imaginary army display made her restless and she moved impatiently. She rose to her elbow and looked toward the heavy curtain that mantled the window. Through a bladelike rift she noted that the moon was not yet gone. Dropping again to her pillow she returned in recollection to Rome, to the court of Tiberius. How many times she had put herself to sleep turning over in her mind the scandals of Julia, the shameless daughter of the emperor! The tangled intrigues of Livia, the queen mother, had often served as a soporific; and to trail some court gossip about Agrippina, the proud and passionate empress, was to follow an easy path to the gates of sleep.

After an hour of fruitless effort that only made her more restive, she sat up in bed.

"Rhoda," she called quietly to the girl. The maid sat up suddenly with the slavish promptness she had cultivated, but she could not dissemble either her anxiety or the weight of sleep that was not to be put off, merely by a change of posture. She rubbed her eyes bewilderedly, and got heavily to her feet, acknowledging the summons with a deep, though uncertain obeisance.

"Rhoda," Procula repeated. The voice was sympathetic, and oddly whimsical. "What do you think of dreams?"

The girl was either too astonished or too sleepy to respond at once, so Procula continued as if in explanation: "Dreams, do you never dream? Do not frights or fancies trouble your head? Or do you Jews dream no more? I heard my master once say the Jews had stopped their silly dreaming since he became their governor."

The slave had had a moment in which to recover from her sudden rousing, and after lighting a tall taper by the bed from the flaxen wick that burned all night out of sight behind a screen, answered modestly:

"Yes, my lady, sometimes I dream. But tonight I have been sleeping too sound for dreaming."

"And what mean the dreams that visit you when your sleep is light?"

"I do not know. There are soothsayers by the city wall in the bazaar of Annas who understand such things. They say that dreams are sometimes the voice of God, and sometimes the voice of the evil one."

"Have you ever visited these men with your dreams?" asked Procula eagerly.

"Nay, my lady," replied the girl with an intimation of embarrassment in her tone. "There are old crones who sell love philters to love-sick maidens, I have been told; but one as young as I should not dream or think of such things. Perhaps when I am older ——"

"Of course; but then, one can hardly help dreaming. Dreams come unbidden to young and old alike. Would you seek the soothsayers if you dreamed a strange and terrible thing?"

"Not I, my lady. I am but a slave girl; and such things are too great for me. I have heard men say that in ancient times armies won victories and rulers were chosen because interpreters of dreams spoke true words of wisdom. And a kitchen maid once told me that every daughter of Abraham dreams she is to bear a king when the first pains of her travail are upon her. But I do not believe such things. Perhaps the dream of bearing a king is the whisper of a midwife to give courage in the hour of pain."

Pilate's wife sat up and hugged her knees to her breast. The slave girl threw a fold of the linen sheet solicitously about her shoulders, against the chill of the early morning. The sound of their conversation had roused one of the guards of Pilate's bedchamber who moved to the door. The two women heard his step, followed by a pause.

"Go part the arras and whisper to him that it is we. Ask him if Pilate sleeps well."

The girl moved noiselessly across the stone floor and did as she was commanded. There was whispered exchange, and when she returned to Procula's bedside she said: "The Procurator has not turned over since midnight."

"I have never borne a child," Procula went on, satisfied with the report of her lord's bovine-like slumber. "But of late I have thrice dreamed of a king. I have no pain to make me dream such things, except it be a pain here." She laid her hand on her heart. "I wonder what a dream-teller would make of it."

The girl made no reply. The light of the taper flared brightly for an instant. The woman turned and looked at it, as if there were a mysterious answer to her question in the leap of flame.

Her dark eyes glowed with impatience. She narrowed them thoughtfully.

"Come hither, child," she said to the girl. "I shall tell you the dream that woke me an hour ago. Sit near me lest our voices disturb the governor's sleep." The girl moved toward her, took the pillow that was offered, and settled herself upon it at the feet of her mistress.

"Strange, it was. I saw a place of death outside the city, beyond the Damascus gate. Three crosses topped a rocky hill, shaped like a skull that grimaced as if in pain." Procula pulled the sheet more securely about her shoulder and shivered. "And as I watched, three men were hung upon the crosses, and a crowd of people set up a great shout, making sport of the suffering victims. And then the cross in the middle began to grow like a tree, only much faster—fast as the little trees the magicians grow under a napkin. It grew, and grew, taller and taller, and the man on it grew larger and larger ——"

She spread her arms out wide as she could to illustrate the cross's growth, and the little girl, watching her intently, said: "See how your arms make great shadows on the wall."

The candle sputtered again, and the woman looked behind her timidly. "There is nothing," she said.

"Nay," answered the slave; "but when you spread your arms ——"

"Oh, I see," Procula resumed. "And the cross and the man upon it grew until they touched the heavens; and the arms of the man seemed to reach out to enfold the earth in an anguished embrace; and wherever the shadow of the cross fell there was blight. And the tip of the cross kept growing till it pierced the heavens and let fall a shaft of light, brighter than the noonday. And then I saw that the places where the dark shadows had fallen were smitten as if by a plague—Rome, Alexandria, Athens, and even the waters of the sea. But, when the light fell from heaven, these stricken places and those who had fallen prostrate and weeping in the shadows, rose again. New cities like alabaster gleamed in the light; and the people danced and sang with new joy. And then the cross was lifted out of its pit and slowly disappeared into the flaming glory of the sun. There was a sound of heavenly music as it was lost to sight. When I looked at the earth again, the two other crosses were turned into beautiful flowering trees, and the place of death was covered with a garden."

She paused, her face alight with wonder and distress. The girl got up and lit a fresh taper. Outside the voice of the watchman announced the fourth watch and the coming of the day. Procula reclined on her elbow for an instant, watching the soundless movements of the slave girl, and then sat up again. Eagerness edged her voice as she spoke excitedly.

"Rhoda, when the day has come, you shall go with my dream to the soothsayers in the booths and learn of them its meaning. I would go myself, but Pilate must not know that my spirit is so sorely troubled."

"But why should such a dream distress you? Is it not fancy, and nothing more?"

"Nay, for it has visited me twice before, and each time the cross grows higher and the man upon it grows greater and the light is more blinding. If I dream it again, the man and the cross will fill the whole earth, and the light will blind me."

"Surely," replied the girl, "such things cannot be. Is it not a dream, this man, this cross, and this light?"

"It is that that I must know. Go to your room now and come again in an hour. Fix my pillow; I shall rest a while until Pilate is awake. When you come back, be ready to go to the bazaar."

The girl bowed low as she went out, but on her face there showed nothing of the resentment and confusion that agitated her heart. She had no wish to go to the booths so early. The streets would be crowded with pilgrims. There would be noise and confusion and brawling around the food stalls. She was unused to such disorder; and held soothsayers and their like in a distrust that was akin to fear.

When she returned to her mistress an hour later, there was very little said between them. Pilate was stirring about in his quarters talking noisily to a soldier who had gained entrance to report a riot in the streets. Procula was anxious to have the girl away on her errand, so putting a leather wallet in her hand, urged her to hurry, and be back as soon as possible with her message. As the girl took leave, there was misgiving in her heart. She scolded herself as she slipped down the dark corridor to the great portal, for having mentioned soothsayers by the city wall.

As she stepped shyly into the street, she was surprised to see the city so lively with early risers. It was not yet the hour for crowds to be abroad; and there was something in the air that was portentous of danger. The great street which led to the Damascus gate was so crowded that she made her way forward with difficulty. A turn to the east offered no easier going. She was annoyed, and then afraid. Her mistress had urged haste, and yet, she reasoned, if the rabble was as thick in the bazaars as in the city streets, there would be little chance of her discharging her duty at all.

She stopped for a moment behind a protecting corner to reconsider her route. Only two or three of the busier streets were familiar to her, so she decided to go back and try the great street again. As she reached the intersection near Pilate's palace whence she had so recently come, she saw a mob of men pressing toward the balcony of the governor's offices. In front of them they shoved a man bound with heavy cords, who, in spite of their jostling and threatening behavior, seemed to move ahead of them in unhurried dignity, as if heedless of their shouting. Rhoda was terrified and the sight of the crowd erased in an instant the commission on which she had been dispatched to the booths. Forgetful of everything save her own safety, she broke and ran like a wild creature. As she sped the distance between the advancing mob and the door to the palace, she heard the rioters shouting, but could make out only one or two words. "King," "crucify" they seemed to yell, and yet she thought, as she pushed into the door that they were strange cries. King, crucify—what could it mean?

She hurried to the chambers of the governor's wife and as she rapped for entrance, she was overcome with the realization that she had miserably failed to do what Procula had so anxiously commanded. Before she could decide what excuse to make, the door opened, and she stood before her mistress.

"Back so soon?" Procula asked her eagerly. For a moment Rhoda couldn't speak. She thought furiously what to say, then penitently replied as she knelt before her:

"Nay, good lady. I couldn't get to the gate. The people are rioting in the streets. They bring a culprit hither to the governor that they may be granted permission to kill him. They shouted so furiously that I could not make out what they said except 'King,' 'crucify.' I was so frightened I came back. When the crowd scatters, I can go to the booths."

To Rhoda's immense relief, there was no rebuke, following her confession. Instead her mistress parted her lips as if about to speak, and then covered her mouth with her hand. From her inner chamber she could dimly hear the noise of the mob outside. Above its sullen murmur she heard voices calling for Pilate. Procula turned toward the rising flood of sound, stopped a moment in indecision and then rushed through the heavy curtains that separated her from the hall leading out to the balcony. As she hurried forward the noise of the people struck her like a blow. She stopped again, and then noticed that Pilate, having heard the disorderly summons, was standing before them on the balcony.

He was no less surprised than the mob when a slave girl suddenly appeared beside him in the bright sunlight. Her eyes were wide with fear and burning with the fire of excitement. She plucked his sleeve and dropped on her knees before him. His heavy face twisted in a scowl of annoyance and he lifted his hand as if to strike her when she said:

"I bring you word from my mistress. She sent me hither to say to you 'Have nothing to do with that innocent man, for during the night I have suffered terribly in a dream through him!' "

Pilate looked from the girl into the darkened corridor. He saw Procula standing, half concealed behind a curtain. She looked at him appealingly, but as he started to speak, disappeared and was gone.

TAKE HIM—CRUCIFY HIM

Pontius Pilate came from the household of Tiberius Caesar in the year A.D. 26 to be procurator over part of the imperial province of Syria, namely: Judea, Samaria, and Idumea. The area was small, about the size of the state of Connecticut; and he was recalled after ten years of almost continuous quarreling with the Jews; and, save for legendary hints, is never again heard from. And yet despite the limited area and time of his procuratorship, his name is one of the most celebrated in history.

Tiberius was, despite the records of his moral aberrations and court intrigues, one of the great rulers of the Roman Empire, by the standard with which his day measured him. As a military commander who added the complete subjugation of the Germanic tribes to his lesser triumphs, a scholar of considerable pretensions, and an administrator whose death left the empire solvent, the people prosperous and the territorial borders secure and peaceful, he deserves higher repute than some of his contemporaries granted him.

One of his favorite maxims concerning the treatment of subject peoples was, "A shepherd should shear his sheep, but never flay them," and his reputation for tolerance in matters religious was notable. It is possible, indeed, that had he not been overly influenced by Sejanus, who became his most trusted minister, and who was violently intolerant of every sort of dissident opinion, the history of Judea during its most fateful period might have been different.

For Pilate was a favorite of Sejanus, and it was through his influence that he was appointed procurator. He was an apt pupil of his important friend at court. The toleration of Augustus Caesar had been odious to the hate-and-fear-haunted Sejanus, and the growth of delation, the darkest shadow that lies on the reign of Tiberius, was mainly a consequence of the malicious encouragement of his minister. Pilate brought to his task a hatred of the Jews, and a skill in the manipulation of intrigue and treachery by which he sought to divide the minds of his subjects, and therefore to make his rule easier.

This is the record of the man who gave Jesus over to death, but it does not entirely account for his heartless act. He was a freedman, one who had either himself or in his immediate ancestry been slave. How he won his title is not known. Money, or some act of notable service to the empire may have achieved the award. But as is often the case, he brought to his office the arrogance that is the compensation one makes for a social stigma. Agrippa described him as "inflexible, merciless, obstinate." Among a subject people whose sense of inviolable freedom extended back as far as the Exodus, it is easy to see how Pilate would appear as an insufferable upstart.

The evidence that the ten short years of his reign provided him with fuel for the fires of revolt is ample; and that he used it is equally so. Beside the profane records there is the word in Luke's gospel (XIII:1) which is typical. "Just at that time people came to tell Jesus about the Galilaeans whose blood Pilate had mingled with their sacrifices." Obviously the Procurator had, by a bloody and contemptuous trick, impressed the pious fools with his idea of ceremonial sacrifice. Nothing, Philo says, so enraged Pilate as an appeal from his judgment to Tiberius; and it was for a singularly cruel and needless slaughter of Samaritans performing a religious act on Mt. Gerizim that Pilate was finally recalled to Rome.

It was such a man before whom Jesus stood. Caiaphas had passed such judgment as was legitimate, though the procedure had violated certain fundamental legal rules. To Pilate, here was another quarrel with his obstinate and fractious subjects. He could not understand them; it was enough that he despised them. If he had known the meaning of much of his distrust of them, he would have recognized it as fear. But fear has a way of seeking disguises for itself, and Pilate, no doubt, had worn them all.

But he was not wholly unaware of what was going on. The record tells us that his prisoner had been remanded to him because of envy. "He knew that it was from envious hatred that Jesus had been brought before him" (Matthew 27:18, Weymouth). How he had found it out is not told, but this judgment of the high priest was clear cut whether or not it was anything else. Obviously Pilate cared little for the alleged breach of the Jewish law with which Jesus was charged. So far as he could ascertain he was guiltless of any matters for which a Roman court could condemn him.

Now ordinarily one might expect that contempt for a people and their holy law, and confidence in the innocence of one accused of its breach would result in release of the accused. If legal, or humane considerations did not suggest release, the wish to spite a law he despised would operate in the prisoner's favor. But the problem was hardly that simple. Here was a subject race. Here was a member of that race who was not only guiltless, but was winsome. But to release him would be to yield to a demand that had been shouted at him from the street, and to yield to a feeling of kindliness toward one of the vassals he despised, was unthinkable. On the contrary, to yield him to death might have two results: it might teach Caiaphas and his crowd what would happen to all pretenders to popular following; and it might put a man out of the way who had ideas about sovereignty, which however fantastic, might prove dangerous.

But more than that. Back behind this local fracas lay a vaster concern. The Jews presented him not only with a problem in provincial administration; they posed also a spiritual problem. They believe in God. Pilate may have thought it foolishness, but it held the potential threat to empire that lives in all proud faith. They believed also in humanity. This to Pilate may have been the silliest sort of sentimentality; but it kept alive the fires in a nation's heart, fires that years of bondage to Rome had not put out. To these two great items of faith, this man before him had testified among the people. Upon love for God and one's neighbor, said he, was suspended the whole framework of their law. And, in order to quicken the minds of his people to the acceptance anew of these great ideals, he had talked about the imminence of a community in which love of God and man would dominate all life. To this Kingdom man's initial and ultimate loyalty belonged.

Of course Pilate believed in none of this nonsense. Tiberius was all the god he knew, and certainly was the only one to whom he owed allegiance. Mankind, to Pilate, was the pawn of empire. The divine Tiberius held the destiny of individual, tribe, or race in his hands. The community in which life was to be endured, was an empire that rested not on worship and the humane spirit, but on law and discipline. Had not Pilate found himself at home in such a cynical and heartless philosophy, Sejanus would never had whispered his recommendation in the emperor's ear. Pilate was in Jerusalem because he hated the Jews. Everything the Jew believed in was repugnant to him. Should he yield to his belief that this one man was guiltless? Should he yield to the frantic warning of his hysterical wife? Should he yield to such humane feelings as played lightly on his stubborn hatred? If he did, he would yield to everything that he despised. How close he skirted the edge of the abyss, over which to plunge was to deny himself and the imperial spirit, is shown in his offer of release of Barabas or Jesus. In retrospect, he must have been glad that the crowd saved him an act of treachery to his own faith.

It was far better from his viewpoint, to let this mild pretender to the leadership of the sons of truth be killed by his own people. He could lend a company of soldiers to this. The envy of the leaders would be both satisfied and chastened. It would teach them a lesson. Their zeal for the integrity of their holy law was envy. It was a sign of their spiritual decadence. "Take him, crucify him!"

This is putting ideas into the mind of Pilate that he would have not recognized, perhaps. So be it. None of us is able to bring into perspective and rationality the part one plays in the drama of destiny. Only as the pages of history slowly turn do we see what use has been made of the greed, the hate, and the envy of men. And, of course the same is to be said for men's heroism, unselfishness, and integrity of soul.

But there is a circumstance in the experience of Jesus that fits this wide canvas on which he and Pilate are so darkly etched. It is, when one reflects upon it, passing strange that Jesus should have spoken of the cross as a possible instrument of his death, and as a personal and voluntary discipline for his followers. Stoning was the death penalty of the Jews; the cross was a Roman device. If Jesus had anticipated that his repudiation by Israel was to go to the lengths of death at their hands, why did he not speak of being stoned? And where is there any intimation that he expected death at the hands of Rome? He never seems to have stirred Roman animosities. He said almost nothing about the Roman Empire, and what he said was commonplace (The great ones of the earth lord it over their fellows), or conciliatory (Render unto Caesar, etc.). Why then did he foresee a Roman cross as the instrument of his death?

His attitude toward his own religion helps us understand

this difficulty. He deplored the lifeless religious formalism of his day, but he believed it could be amended and restored. Indeed he predicted, not its abrogation, but its universalization. "Not one jot or tittle will pass away until it all be fulfilled." To this great faith the answer was not likely to be a volley of stones, and a cairn over the battered body of the victim.

But, of Rome he could never have said, "no jot nor tittle shall pass away till it all be fulfilled." For Rome was to him the antithesis of Israel. Its worship of an emperor-deity was blasphemous; its derogation of all the human dignities to the service and aggrandizement of empire was insufferable; its dream of world dominion pressed forward by the edge of the sword was the abomination of desolation. With that there could be no compromise, and an intransigent spirit was the mark of piety. If death was to be the issue of his ministry, it would be death on the cross. If those who shared his ideals would share his destiny, they too must refuse to compromise with the philosophy of empire, and they too must bear their own crosses. In the long light of history the cross was the answer of the idea of empire to the idea of the beloved community. That it has become the symbol of resignation and even of gentleness (the Red Cross, e.g.) is one of the mysteries of the ages, except that we have come at last to see that only as that cross and that issue are voluntarily accepted can life, as we know it, be redemptive.

Jesus, the emissary of God, the exemplar of love, the agent of redemption, confronted Pilate, the pupil of Sejanus who feared and hated the Jews, the representative of Tiberius whose empire balanced always on the thin Etruscan blade of a Roman sword. Rome's answer to him was inevitably: "Take him, crucify him." Not even the clairvoyance of the governor's wife could change the issue.

It is this single and significant fact that should sharpen the focus of the Christian mind on the recrudescence of this conflict in our own times. However feeble may have been the testimony of Israel to the ideal of the beloved community, and however poorly some Jews we know may have exemplified it (the same thing is true about Christians who share the tradition and neglect it!) the fact remains that the ideal is Jewry's great gift to human life and thought. Her great prophets foretold it, her greatest son died for it. And it still lives, unabridged and unchanged, in the heart of humanity.

And obviously it stands in direct conflict with every other social or political ideology that thinks in terms of a derogation of God, man, and society, to human ends. It is this that accounts for the reappearance of anti-Semitism in our day. It is nearly always true that the emergence of a great new secular social ideal results in facing up to the Hebrew ideology of the Kingdom of God. And if the secular order violates the rudiments of the Kingdom ideal, the authors and sustainers of this ideal through the ages are accused of seeking the destruction of the newcomer. It is not so stated in the newspapers. When Mr. Hitler says the Jew must go from modern Germany, he explains that it was the betrayal of the republic, the manipulation of national and international finance, the monoply of the professions, the indirect control of industry and what not, that compelled his anti-Semitism. But granted all this to be true—which it obviously is not—Hitler could live with it. He has made terms with the same thing under what he calls Aryan domination. What he says, whether he knows it or not, is that he cannot exploit his idea of totalitarianism and racial dominion without confronting the deathless dream of a world community based on God, and a just, equal and brotherly society. The Jews gave that to the world, and the only way, in the secular view, to get rid of it, is to get rid of the Jews.

The amazing and tragic fact is that the Christians of the world regard anti-Semitism as something apart from them. To so misunderstand the modern conflict is to turn our backs on a great tradition that is as truly ours as it is the Jews'; and in remaining persistently blind to its implications for the world at large, to invite the ultimate repudiation of Christendom by the modern imperialist mind.

So stands Christ before Pilate at this fateful hour!

It may be that once again it is the tension of our stressful days that has given shape to the anti-Semitism that increases throughout the earth. We remind ourselves that much that took place in and around Jerusalem during the days of our Lord's Passion finds partial explanation in the inflamed and irritable tempers of men. Pilate was disdainful and afraid. Caiaphas was envious and anxious. Procula dreamed wildly, and the mob was restive. The possibility of other things having happened invites interesting but futile speculations; but this we can truly know: unless the tensions of our day are some-how loosened, anything may happen.

History is reluctant that her great should die. So where there is no record to supply immortality, legend provides it. Concerning Pilate, stories have arisen that keep his memory fresh in a fascinating way. It was the historian Eusebius who gave space to the story that Pilate, because of the fires of anti-Roman hatred that his abuse of the Jews caused, was first recalled to Rome, and then exiled to Gaul. His exile carried with it a sentence of death which he was required to execute by his own hand. So, the tale runs, he committed suicide, and his body was cast into the Rhone. So greatly were the waters disturbed that the corpse was driven north into "Losania" where it was plunged into the gulf near Lucerne and below Mt. Pilatus. Every Good Friday it is raised from the lake, to sit and endlessly wash its unavailing hands until the night comes. Others say that if one speaks over the place where the body rests, it will come to the surface, and beg for sympathy with staring, vacuous eyes.

Such tales are only mildly interesting, and yet sometimes

they have startling pertinence. Pilate has appeared so recently in so many places that one suspects his body came to rest in every country in the old world. Lucerne holds him in no custody. He is bold to go wherever he likes. And of late he has lost his obsequious and apologetic manner. He does not wash his hands. He seems not to hear the execrations of the centuries heaped upon his cowardly head. He has walked in glory to the capitals of the world, and been welcomed in their chancellories. He understands the words he hears. The anguished warning of Procula is lost in the acclaim of uniformed men. It is a threatening and ominous sound. It is the challenge of empire to the Beloved Community again.

Dr. Arthur E. Holt in the *Christian Century* of August 23, 1939 wrote: "The World War and the attempted solutions by all the national 'isms' have convinced me that the need for this community of the Spirit is more imperative than ever. Men are seeking security in practical absolutes like those of race or nationality or culture, and all this but reveals the necessity for something which will save them from their ethical provincialism and temper their petty prides and hates. Break any one of these new national orders open and you will find that it is a struggle over the stuff of which religion is made. The world has suddenly turned religious but most of its gods are false . . . and so I am thrown back to my belief that the community of the spirit alone possesses what modern society needs."

Six days that changed the direction of human history. They seem to return to us again. What are we to say: "Have nothing to do with that innocent man, for during the night I have suffered terribly in a dream through him"? We can well afford to be troubled by him again. Or shall we join with Pilate to say: "Take him, let him be crucified"?

CONCLUSION

These shared his passion but not his poise. The word passion is a derivative of a root which means "to suffer." If today it means excitement or intensity of feeling, so much the worse for language. It is important, however, that we be reminded that excitement or intensity of feeling is not, of itself, significant. As has been pointed out in these pages, Jesus constantly sought to slacken the tempo of his feelings. One night he spent at Bethany, or perhaps two; but after that, only the solace of a garden could quiet his racing heart. But he did win; and when he was finally in possession of himself, he could speak with gentleness when his friends faltered, walk with dignity when his enemies menaced, and maintain a silence, majestic and accusing, when insult and threat were offered him.

But he made no effort to escape pain; and herein lies an important difference between him and those who shared his passion. Their disquiet, running all the way from inquisitiveness to panic, was born of a wish to escape the pain that the logic of events promised them. In so far as they shared his passion, it was in the effort to escape the very thing for which he was nerving himself.

Some of the manifold varieties of fear have engaged us through these pages. Martha's attitude toward Mary was not unmixed with fear—it was jealousy, perhaps; but jealousy is a compound of ambition and anxiety. Thomas was afraid. What is more surely productive of fear than the sense of being lost—not knowing where one is going? Philip was afraid. What is more terrifying to one who has been nurtured in a profound faith in God, than to discover that God is gone? Peter was afraid, gripped by a primitive and disintegrating terror; Judas was afraid, dulled by a sense of frustration and a knowledge that his hopes for himself were doomed. And Pilate feared an ideal that is the Nemesis of all imperialisms.

How much a psychosis of fear is responsible for the present disorder in the modern world, has been hardly more than hinted at here. Much is being said about the conquest of this irresponsible mood; but one wonders whether the mind of the hour is yet ready to listen to the instruction it needs. For us, the formula of John the Elder, or Jesus' word to Simon Peter by the sea, is still the answer to our anguished spirits.

But we must not make the mistake of thinking that the mere intensity of feeling that characterizes our life is the sort of passion our Lord endured. "Love is an agony," said St. Augustine. Passion is suffering, not to escape suffering, but to make itself redemptive. In this way the eternal relevance of the cross illumines the last six days of the Savior's life. Those who shared his passion knew not its essential meaning, for he was sharing the passion of eternity. This is why their passion betrayed them into defeat, and why his passion led him to victory. He was the lamb, slain from the foundation of the world.

Life is essentially tragic. This is no morbid word. Life begins in a paroxysm of physical anguish, and ends in the pains of death. This is no surrender to pessimism, for birth pangs are redemptive and death pangs are the prelude to ineffable triumph. The unique quality of human life—indeed its only divine endowment, we incline to say—is the capacity to make the tragedy of life redemptive; to transmute the pain of mortal life into the power of godlikeness.

These are admittedly trying days. The hearts of millions are shaken by fear, and tortured by anxious questions. To the secularist there is no answer but despair, or a desperate and uncalculating frenzy of self-protection. But to the Christian who has apprehended the meaning of the Cross, these days may be the overture of a new Redemption, which shall ultimately be made possible only by those, who down the ages and to the end of time, have shared and will share the passion of the Son of Man.